SWING LIKE YOU DON'T CARE

MIND FITNESS FOR EXQUISITE GOLF

Arnie Kozak, Ph.D.

To all golfers of the past who helped to create this great game and all the golfers of the present who aspire to get better

Published by Exquisite Mind Press
Burlington, Vermont
Asheville, North Carolina

ISBN-10: 1660122783
ISBN-13: 978-1660122783

arniekozak.com

Table of Contents

PREFACE 7

ACKNOWLEDGEMENTS 7

FORWARD 9

INTRODUCTION 12

MIND TRAINING 15

1. Mind Fitness 15
2. Too Many Minds 19
3. Sensory Clarity 21
4. If You're Not Breathing, Your Handicap is the Least of Your Problems 23
5. I Remember Now That I have Forgotten 25
6. Wi-Fi 26
7. You Can't Think Your Way Out of a Problem Thinking Got You into in the First Place 29
8. Beware the Fine Print 31
9. Fierce Attention 34

NEUROSCIENCE 37

10. Going Unconscious 37
11. 100:1 39
12. Amy G. Dala 41
13. Mirror, Mirror on the Wall 43
14. See the Shot; Be the Shot 44
15. 10,000 Hours or 10 Years, Whichever Comes First 49
16. Tiger's Tibia 51

17. Cool-Mad 54

SPORT PSYCHOLOGY 57

18. Perfectomy 57

19. The Inner Light 60

20. Please Leave Your Ego, With Your Shoes, At the Door 61

21. Freedom is Nothing More Than Telling Shame and Death to Go %#*! Themselves 66

22. Why Didn't I Kneel More Deeply to Accept You? 70

23. Stress is an Orange: Juice It! 72

24. Different Day Different Body 78

25. The Whole is Greater than the Sum of the Parts 81

26. Don't Take Yourself So Seriously 83

27. Violent Emotion is a Kind of Insanity 84

28. Go With The Flow! 88

GOLF TECHNIQUE 90

29. Kill Hope 90

30. Normal Curve 93

31. Frustration = Variation x Resistance 95

32. Death Grip 97

33. Set Up and Shut Up (or If You Think; You'll Stink) 99

34. Your Wish is My Command 101

35. Slice Virus 103

36. The Ultimate Shot 105

37. Right Practice 106

38. Swing Like You Don't Care 110

WISDOM 113

39. If You Aim at Your Target You've Already Missed 113
40. The Antidote to Exhaustion is Not Necessarily Rest 115
41. No Thank You 117
42. Thank You 119
43. Then They Still Have You in Prison 122
44. Watching the Grass Grow 123
45. Equanimi-Tee 125
46. Be Thine Own Caddy 127
47. Sweat When You're Hot; Shiver When You're Cold; Shank When You're Tense 129
48. The Great (Golf) Way is Not Difficult for Those Who Have No Preferences 131
49. April Moon 132
50. The Sharp Edge of a Razor is Difficult to Pass Over; Thus, The Wise Say the Path to Salvation is Hard 133
51. The Perfect Doubt 134
52. Opening the Gate 135
53. Take Off Your Shoes 136
54. 54 137

AFTERWORD 139

APPENDIX 140

Overview: Mind Fitness Practices 140

Theme One: Focus on The Positive 142

Theme Two: Acceptance 142

Theme Three: Ground Attention in the Present 143

Theme Four: Find Peace in the Midst of the Storm *143*
Theme Five: Ride the Wave of Change *144*
MIND FIT PRACTICES 144
Seated *144*
Seated into Standing *146*
Standing *146*
Slow Motion Drill *147*
Diaphragmatic Breathing *147*
Body Scan *148*
Walking *148*
Putting *149*
Playing *149*
FOOTNOTES **151**
WORKS CITED **180**

PREFACE

Swing Like You Don't Care: Mind Fitness for Impeccable Golf is a practical field manual for taking your game to the next level. Like Harvey Penick's, *The Little Red Book*, you can put this book on your iPhone or in your back pocket and carry with you on the course for reference. As with my book *108 Metaphors for Mindfulness*, this book looks to metaphor, analogy, and story to bring elusive golf concepts to life. The images presented on the pages to follow will help you to understand your golf game and, by extension, your life in heartfelt ways. You can read these entries straight through or you can skip around. For best results, read it all the way through once and then stick it in your pocket for quick reference when the need arises!

ACKNOWLEDGEMENTS

This book was shaped and inspired by all my golfing friends, colleagues, and mentors. I will always think of Steve "Gonzo" Gonsalves first in this regard. He gave me my first golf lessons and has been a great supporter and friend ever since. I am also indebted to the professional golfers that I have had the fortune to train. Special thanks to Todd Trono, Vermont PGA Player of the Year 2005 to 2008, for his openness, tough questions, and inquisitive mind. Andrew Pfister was an early supporter and took to my methods like a duck takes to water. My golf students deserve special thanks with special mention to Jory Curran and Deb Fletcher. The marriage between golf and my professional work was so obvious and implicit that it took another professional to point it out to me! I thank Nancy Silberg for doing so.

This project could not have proceeded without the wisdom of my dharma friend and mentor Shinzen Young for teaching me about the structure of the mind and for the teachings that form the basis of Mind Fitness.

Another special thanks go to my friend the artist, Erik Odin Cathcart, who designed the Exquisite Mind Golf website and provided early encouragement of this project. His vision of the silver tee appears throughout this manuscript.

My golf-specific personal trainer, Scott Bevins, has helped me to refine my workouts to support my golf swing and provided a physical confidence that propels me forward.

My golfing buddy, Steele Taylor, for showing me what a golf swing looks like and for the hours of pleasurable play. Thanks also to all the friends and strangers that I've walked the links with special mention to Sam Standard, Jay Hoffman, Gavin Mills, and Richard and Flo Damon.

Dr. Tyler Nelson, one of my oldest and dearest friends, has nurtured my love of golf and provided me with access to his home course where I first figured out how to play this game in some way resembling elegance, if only glancingly

FORWARD

> It is nothing new or original to say that golf is played one stroke at a time. But it took me many years to realize it.—Bobby Jones

Each time I see a youth golfer making a great swing, or even a not so great swing, I get wistful and wonder what might have happened had I played golf as a child. Unfortunately, I did not pick up a golf club until I was 32 years old, and the clubs I picked up were culled from garage sales. They were a mongrel group of persimmon woods and rusty irons, some of which, I later discovered, were lady's clubs. I toted them around in a strapless turquoise and black trim vinyl bag with a single pocket, its zipper broken. I think the price tag for the whole lot was $8. When I turned 40, I made an impulse purchase of a set of Golden Bear Jack Nicklaus signature clubs from Costco. This was an impulse purchase not because the clubs were expense but because I played golf only once per year, usually at the company retreat. The season I bought the clubs, I probably played 3 times—a big year for me. A couple of years later I received my first pair of golf shoes for my 42nd birthday. I remember trying them out for the first time. It was a warm early summer evening in Vermont, and I was playing at a local course—The Links at Lang Farm. I was walking down the 12th fairway leading to a green that disappears into the woods. It's a lovely sight, and I thought to myself I might actually enjoy playing golf. At the time, I had no illusions of being good. The next year, I played more than I ever had before. In the Fall, I hit the links in Napa while I was out there for a wedding, and then I played in North Carolina in December. This extended season brought me to somewhere close to ten rounds. I still didn't think I was good or might even be good, although at times I could hit the ball well. During this season, a friend of mine wondered if I was applying my mindfulness expertise to my golf game and whether I was planning to develop a clinic to help others. I had been applying mindfulness to my own game, naturally, but not explicitly. I hadn't thought of teaching others until she asked.

I consider my 44th year to be my first real season of playing golf. I played and practiced regularly and took my first lessons. I had the temerity and fortune to approach Steve "Gonzo" Gonsalves, Head PGA Professional at the Links at Lang Farm. I took a series of lessons from Steve. In our first lesson, he asked me to hit some wedge shots. I did so with a mixture of nervousness and violence. He let me hack away for a few strokes and then smiled broadly and said, "I can help you; this is going to be easy." He straightened out and readjusted my grip and stance; things started to fall in place. He had me lighten my swing. "80% effort Doc," he chided. After hitting wedges with a relative degree of grace, he asked me to pull out my 7-iron. Under his careful tutelage, something seemingly magical started to happen. My 7-irons were going nearly 200 yards. In 20 years of teaching, he had never seen this. "Damn, I could be good!" Now I thought I might be good. While taking my lessons with Steve, I pitched him my idea to do a clinic on using sport psychology and mindfulness principles in golf. He was very open and graciously supported my debut clinic in September 2007 and, thus, Exquisite Mind Golf was born.

The following year I suffered from the illusion that not only could I be good, I could be *really* good. I had yet to break 90 yet already saw myself as a scratch golfer, heading to the Champions Tour as soon as I turned 50. This was the first season I kept a handicap and, as of Memorial Day weekend, I had played almost as much that season as I did the previous one. By the end of the six-month short Vermont season, I had logged about 50 rounds in between my teaching, clinical, and writing commitments. I had lowered my handicap by 5.3 strokes. I did so by using the Exquisite Mind Golf techniques presented in this book. Staying in the present, getting out of my own way, and enjoying the game helped me to be relaxed and to play in an increasingly effective way. That season, I also read the informative and entertaining memoir *Paper Tiger*. Golf writer Thomas Coyne attempts to qualify for the PGA tour by taking one year of his life to prepare. I don't think one year is enough, especially for someone like him who hadn't played serious golf for almost ten years. When I tell people that I'll be ready for the Champions Tour, this always gets a chuckle. It's not funny though; I *could* do it, I thought, and I had five years to get there! Now, my 50th birthday is approaching and I am not quite ready for the Tour. My handicap has continued to lower each season as I work on my game. Playing golf has been a great teacher. I've lowered my handicap by more than half from its initial register in the low 30s. As of this writing, I am a 14 and on the verge of becoming a scratch golfer. Hope springs eternal!

The final nail in my Champion's Tour fantasy was Vijay Singh. The year he won the FedEx Cup, I realized that we were the same age, which meant that no matter how good I got I'd have to play against him on tour. One season at a time is a better approach. My aim is to become impeccable on the golf course, and to do so I will have to embrace, embody, and engage all the knowledge, wisdom, and practical advice in the forthcoming pages.

INTRODUCTION

> Unfortunately, the single most important fact about golf is as calming as a digital prostate exam. It's hard. Ridiculously hard, if your goal is to play well.—Carl Hiaasen

To learn a new skill, we accept the fact that we must train. We must put in the time and effort, whether it's a musical instrument, a foreign language, or any other complex task, including golf—especially golf. However, we tend to take our own minds for granted; we don't see the same need to train psychological faculties like attention in the same way we need to train lag putting and lob wedging. This is a surprising fact of being human: our most intimate sense of mind appears to be everywhere and under our control, but this is an illusion. Conscious attention is like a flashlight in a dark room, everywhere the flashlight "looks" appears to be bright. Likewise, everywhere our attention "looks" the mind appears to be conscious and thereby in control. Because of the familiarity of conscious attention, we don't see the need to train it formally. I ask all of my students about their history of paying attention: "We were all expected to pay attention in school; were you ever shown how to do it?" I am still waiting for an affirmative answer.

A simple demonstration will show how your mind is out of control. Pick an object to focus on and then make it your intention to give this object your full attention. Try this now. How long is it before thoughts, images, or feelings encroach on this attention? One second? Two seconds? Five seconds? If you are like most people, your mind cannot follow the simple instruction of paying attention to an object of its own choosing for more than a few moments. In this sense, our minds are undisciplined, out of shape—having the equivalent of a beer-gut. Fortunately, there are methods that can train the mind. These methods are straightforward, even simple, yet not always easy to implement. The mind is very accustomed to having its own way and may resist the invitation to become focused. The axioms, maxims, and metaphors in this book will show you why and how to train the mind. They'll teach you how to get out of your own way so you can enjoy golf more and play the best game that you have.

Golf, perhaps more than any other game, relies upon psychology. Estimates range to golf being 90 percent mental. Think about it, the ball is stationary; the target is stationary; no opponents interfere with the execution of the shot. It is body and mind against the laws of physics, and physics so often wins. At the moment of making a swing, our mental state is critical to the shot's outcome. Wholehearted attention will allow the body to do what it knows how to do. This quality of attention—that swings like it doesn't care—will bring the best results that are possible given your current level of skill and help to take your game to the next level.

The fifty-four chapters of this book are organized around five themes. The first section, Mind Training, describes Mind Fitness as it applies to life and golf. The second section, Neuroscience, cites brain research to teach us important lessons about the game. The next section, Sport Psychology, covers the findings of this field as they apply to golf. The following section, Golf Technique, provides practical tips and guidance on how to improve your game. The final section focuses upon philosophical virtues drawn from wisdom traditions as they apply to golf and life beyond golf.

Harry Vardon suggested, "Perfect confidence and a calm mind are necessary for the success of every stroke." He also cautioned the golfer "not to be morbid." The wisdom and practical advice on the pages to follow will help you to embody this perfection—without getting perfectionistic—and to play with a calm mind, no matter the circumstances. The success of every stroke is guaranteed if you come to it in the right frame of mind.

By training the mind as these chapters suggest, you can learn to "swing like you don't care." That is, you can learn to swing naturally without tension and the disruptive force of desire. You can bring golf and life together as a path of learning, one that feels deep and meaningful. By shifting your attitudes, you can enjoy the great game of golf and play the best game that you have every time that you play.

MIND TRAINING

This section explores the structure and dynamic functioning of the mind and how we can work with it better—making it more responsive, nimble, and cooperative. We can think of mind training as a precise inner science with identifiable components and processes. We can use our minds to focus exactly on what is happening in the moment. We can also use our minds to generate positive states, even when things are not going well. We can focus on the calm in the midst of a storm and the storm itself—shifting from seeing it as trouble to a series of changing experiences. We'll explore the concept of *mind fitness* and other metaphors that map out the challenges we face in managing our attention and self-image while playing golf. This section will lay the foundation for the remaining axioms, maxims, and metaphors. The goal is to know our minds *intimately*. The more familiar we become, the more freedom we will enjoy, even as we counterintuitively move closer to the things that challenge us the most.

1. Mind Fitness

To get the body fit, we run, lift weights, and eat healthful food. How then to get the mind fit? Mind fitness is an attainable goal when we can get beyond the illusion that the mind is already in shape. As our most basic sense of self, the mind can seem to be responsive, focused, and fit. However, any close inspection reveals the mind to be none of these. Attention is a faculty that unless specifically trained will not be fit, focused, and responsive. To perform optimally in golf, we need our minds to be ready and able to perform. Being familiar with the mind can help us to maximize its potential. Let's take a structured look at the mind to find out how and what to train.

Let's start with a topographical map of the mind where we can identify both internal (subjective) and external (objective) components. The objective components of mind include sight and sound—sensory experiences that are always with us (even when our eyes are closed we are seeing shades of light). Touch or tactile sensations in the body are also always present. To a less frequent degree, we experience smells and tastes but no so much when we are golfing. The subjective components of mind include feelings, mental images, and self-talk. These three—*feel, image and talk— FIT*—are the features of Mind Fitness or Mind *FIT*ness. "Feel" is any bodily-based feeling with emotional flavoring—pleasant, unpleasant, and neutral. Feel-space can occur anywhere in the body. Of course, feel is crucial to the golf swing. "Image" are all the pictures or scenes that appear in the mind's viewing screen as if behind the eyes. "Talk" is any component of thought that has words. If we think about it for a minute, we will notice that most of our mental life takes place in talk-space. The mind components of Feel-Image-Talk (FIT) can occur individually or in the combinations of Feel-Image, Feel-Talk, Image-Talk, or Feel-Image-Talk. Golf requires the following: a Feel-Image (FI) of the upcoming shot and a Talk-Image (TI) that helps set up the shot before and then is quiet during the shot.

It's easy to see how the activity of FIT in any given moment can be a benefit or detriment to your golf game. Nervousness and negative self-talk kill performance. Images of the ball going out of bounds or into the hazard can, as if by magic, bring about the feared result. A relaxed, confident swing will achieve better results. If we don't point FIT in helpful directions, our game will suffer. Mind Fitness, then, trains our minds to fit, responsive, and concentrated.

What is it, exactly, that gets FIT? This something is the capacity for awareness. We can experience the mind as a collection of contents—the meanings of feelings, images, stories—or we can experience the mind as a process—a ceaseless flow of feelings, images, and talk, that is being aware that the mind is talking without getting caught up in what the mind is saying. The process mode doesn't care why the stories are there; it simply notices they are occurring. To get FIT, we train this awareness so that attention can be responsive when we need it to be. We train it to be cooperative—to have feelings, images, and talk that facilitate playing excellent golf. We train it to be compliant—to be quiet when we need it to be quiet and to be active when we need it to be active. Without such training, we are at the whim of the mind. This mind tries its best to steer the brain, the most complex thing in the known universe. Sometimes it seems like the mind is a drunken bus driver, running over curbs, hurtling to disaster. Rather than leaving outcomes to chance, we can work with the mind. This is Mind Fitness.

Concentration is natural outcome of a FIT mind. When we hear the term concentration, we may think of one type of concentration—single-pointed focus. A more fruitful definition for concentration, however, is paying attention to what is deemed most relevant in any given moment. By this definition, concentration may be narrowly focused or broadly focused depending on the situation. In golf, we need to maintain a fluid sense of concentration. Often, we'll need to keep a broad view and focus upon the requirements for our swing and the context in which this swing is about to happen. "What is the lie?" "What are the wind and other conditions that may affect this shot?" No two shots are exactly the same and would therefore require different types of concentration. Complex tasks, such as those we execute playing golf, require broad, relaxed consideration of the available information, internal and external. Indeed, "being distracted from relevant information by irrelevant information is the cause of the huge variations in performance."

One day on my home course, I pushed my tee shot on the par 3 10th a little short and to the right. I collected myself and executed an excellent second. Unfortunately the ball sat 30 feet from the hole. I looked at my feet and the ball was sitting exactly where I asked it to go. However, this was not where it needed to go. I was concentrated on my swing but neglected my alignment. Attention should be a wide sky, and when we golf we should devote the mind to all the factors relevant to this shot, including the features of the lie, the conditions of the ground, the wind, and any other factors that are relevant—including our alignment to the target!

Concentration, like attention or any other faculty, is a trainable skill. Mind Fitness will raise our level of concentrative power, just as running will raise our level of aerobic fitness. Unlike sports such as football, basketball, and baseball, the golfer appears to be in control. No one is attempting to tackle us, steal the ball, or slide a fastball by at 100 m.p.h. The ball is stationary and waits for us. We bring to each shot our physical skills and knowledge of the game. We'd be able to play impeccably if we could concentrate impeccably. No matter what level you are at, it is difficult to play with consistency. Mind Fitness can help to minimize inconsistency. The FIT mind must filter external information and manage internal distractions. The more we practice training the mind, the more we can do this effortlessly.

Can you get your mind in sufficient shape enough to be resolutely concentrated for the 1.7 seconds required to execute a golf swing? If you multiply 1.7 seconds by the number of shots you need to take in a given round, this doesn't amount to much—perhaps 2 or 3 minutes of pure concentration. Can you be unwavering for that long? Can you expand your steadfast focus to include the entire pre-shot routine—now add 5 to 10 seconds to however many shots you take? Gradually, you can make the entire round into a Mind Fitness training session where you move into and out of focus at will. The FIT mind is nimble and responsive to the requests made of it. You'll be able to request it to focus on this next shot—impeccable, implacable, and immovable.

2. Too Many Minds

If you've paid any attention to your own mind, you've noticed that it likes to talk a lot. This is the "talk" of Mind Fitness. We all do this. We all have minds that tend to wander into the future and the past telling stories and having conversations. We all have minds that comment about what's happening now. This is the *Storytelling Mind.* Unfortunately, much of this Storytelling Mind activity is unnecessary at best and destructive at worst. How often, though, are we giving our full attention to what is actually happening now? Chances are that our minds are talking during our golf swing. If we're lucky, the conversation will at least be about golf instead of something else. Even this golf talk can be a hindrance. You can't think and swing well at the same time. In every moment, you have a choice: you can be with the content or you can be with the process. The golf mind excels when it sticks to the process and becomes bogged down when it gets caught up in content. Which mind will you bring to your next game?

William James, one of the founders of American psychology, said, "The intellectual life of man consists almost wholly in his substitution of a conceptual order for the perceptual order in which his experience originally lives." Great golf is played within the perceptual order rather than the conceptual order. Life, too, is truly lived in perceived experience, rather than thinking about those experiences. The way we are wired, however, tends to push us towards the conceptual order over the perceptual order unless we deliberately practice getting to know the perceptual order.

George Plimpton tells a wonderful story of his spontaneous "discovery" of Mind Fitness. He does so the morning before he is to participate in a round of the Bing Crosby at Cypress Point. Taking a tip from Walter Hagen who would get himself into a state of "controlled languor" in which he would "shave very slowly, work his toothbrush up and down with careful patience, [and] his breakfast would be a lengthy affair." This unhurried attitude provided a metaphor for the golf shot. Not to hurry and not to get "quick." Plimpton attempts to recreate this approach. To do so, he had to turn away from his Storytelling Mind: "I stepped outside and ambled very slowly down to the lodge dining room. My hands smoked (from soaking them in very hot water, a Gene Sarazen tip), I looked carefully at the flowerbeds and the shrubbery. My head moved as slowly as a turret. It was Hagen, after all, who had given the memorable piece of advice about going down a fairway which was applicable not only to golf but to just about anything: 'Along the way,' he had said, 'be sure to take the time to smell the flowers."

Plimpton carries on with Mind Fitness eating. Over breakfast, he gives his complete attention to eating. As is natural, the process slows down so that each moment can be appreciated. In his own words: "I dawdled over the grapefruit. I raised the spoon. I felt my teeth pop slowly into the skin of the fruit and I felt the spray of the juice hit against the roof of my mouth. The sensation was astonishing: taste considered in such reflection was almost overpowering. The mind boiled. I turned to the toast. Slowly I scraped a knife with some butter on it across the toast—spreading it evenly. Then came the honey. I opened the container carefully and dipped the knife into the honey and spread it on the toast. The eating was interesting the—the juxtaposition of butter and honey, the difference in consistency, just the slightest, so that one could lose oneself in contemplation."

As we can see from his detailed description, this mind FIT eating took some time. Unfortunately for him, he got lost in the process. "I brought my arm up slowly and looked at my watch. My blood jumped. It was later than I thought possible." Perhaps it's best not to practice such mind FIT eating with an early tee time looming! He then describes the complete deterioration of his Mind Fitness as he rushes to the golf course, gets lost, becomes frantic, and finally arrives at his destination with moments to spare.

Any activity can be Mind Fitness when the Storytelling mind becomes quiet. Learning how to quiet this mind is the central work of Mind Fitness.

3. Sensory Clarity

Life is more vivid in the present moment. What would happen if we gave our full attention to what is happening right now? Have you ever noticed that the grass is greener and the sky bluer when you are in the "zone"? Have you ever noticed that you notice more when the conversations in your mind are quiet? If we are involved in such conversations, it's hard to really notice what is going on around us. If we are engaged in inner commentary—storytelling— it is as if a veil has been placed over our experience, making it difficult to make contact with what is there. Mind Fitness training can help to lift that veil. Clarity can be thought of as the ability to keep track of the components of your sensory experience as they arise in various combinations, moment-by-moment.

What are the advantages of having such clarity? How could it benefit your golf game? Golf is a game that requires sensory clarity. We must be able to see the course to anticipate how to make our next shot. We must be able to feel the shot, and this requires a finely tuned bodily awareness of feel. Arnold Palmer emphasized that the right feel might mean adjusting the swing just a couple of centimeters.

The FIT mind is attuned to its surroundings and unburdened by distractions. Sensory clarity is a by-product of concentration. We can cultivate this awareness by practicing it out on the course. Golfing offers an array of enticing sensory experiences. See the different colors and textures of the grass as you walk between holes. Listen to the sounds around you—those generated by nature and humans. Regard these sights and sounds with interest. If your mind starts to tell stories about them, bring attention back to the sensory qualities that you can see and hear—the varying shades of green, the trees, the lakes, and the entire panorama of visual delight. Notice any smells that arise as you breathe in the fresh air. As you move in your body, observe the touch sensations that arise. This is likely to be a pleasurable experience. You might even be surprised at the details you notice, even in familiar places.

When we emerge from the clouds that can occupy the mind, we find ourselves in the present moment in all its wonder. This can be an awe-inspiring experience that helping us to appreciate the experience of golf independent of the score for that round.

4. If You're Not Breathing, Your Handicap is the Least of Your Problems

To train the mind we need to have some object to focus upon. Any object would do. We could choose a special sound, a candle flame, or a spot on the wall. However, focusing on breathing brings certain advantages. Breathing is always happening; you can't forget to bring it with you. As I tell my students, "If you're not breathing, your handicap is the least of your problems." Breathing is natural and automatic and always happens now. By focusing attention on breathing, we are focusing attention on the present moment, and this is where mind training pays its dividends. How we breathe also reflects our emotional state. When we are tense and anxious, breathing may become rapid and shallow. When we are relaxed, breathing tends to be soft and slow.

The first step for Mind Fitness breathing is not to breathe in any particular way. The instructions are to allow your breathing to be natural without interference. Focus your attention on the physical aspects of the breathing experience. When your attention wanders—which it will do, perhaps as soon as a second or two after starting—refocus your attention. That's the exercise. Focus, get distracted, notice you've become distracted, then refocus. Simple. Concentrate on your breathing and when attention wanders bring it back and start over again. There's one caveat. When you bring your attention back, give yourself permission to do so without berating yourself for the fact that your mind wandered. All minds wander. It's no big deal. Repeat this process over and over again.

Another opportunity is to develop *interest* in what is happening now with the breath. This interest seeks to greet the breathing process where it is rather than to impose some agenda on the experience. See if your mind is imposing expectations. Perhaps it wants to become "relaxed" because that is what your mind thinks breathing should be all about. See what happens if you give up this striving. Having said this, relaxation is a reliable by-product of this breathing exercise but not its goal. If relaxation happens—wonderful—enjoy that. If relaxation doesn't happen, can you be interested in what *does* happen?

Awareness of breathing is crucial on the course. When we are tense, we actually may hold our breath during the golf swing. How is that going to work out? Instead of holding your breath, use it as an ally during the swing. I make sure that I inhale as I take my back swing and exhale when I come forward. As an added bonus, swinging on the exhalation introduces power into the swing. You can also visualize by imagining the breath coming into and leaving from the shaft of the club. Experiment with different ways of breathing. The key is to keep breathing natural—without tension.

Once you have established the foundation of breathing naturally with awareness, it can help to develop the habit of breathing with your diaphragm—the wall of muscle at the bottom of the lungs. When the diaphragm is engaged, breathing is deep and generates relaxation. To check whether your diaphragm is active, place one hand on your belly and the other on your chest. As you breathe, only your lower hand should be moving. Practice breathing diaphragmatically when you are off the course. The more you practice, the more natural this way of breathing will become.

5. I Remember Now That I have Forgotten

> "How are you getting on with that memory-training course you got by correspondence?" "I'm improving. Now I can sometimes remember that I have forgotten something."

We mostly live our lives asleep. As one psychologist observed, it is as if we are in mutually agreed upon trance. We can move through life on automatic pilot. Moments, hours, days, weeks, months, and years can pass by unexamined without much awareness. An entire lifetime can go by if we're not careful. Inviting Mind Fitness into our lives helps us to see how asleep we have been and gives us the chance to wake up. Even still, at first, we will continue to be on automatic pilot most of the time. After all, it has taken many years of conditioning to become so automatic and these habits will not die quickly. Remembering that we are forgetting is an important first step in the process of change. These moments of awareness that pop-up during the day and on the course speak to another way of being. When we remember, we re-*member* ourselves, that is, connect with our breathing bodies in this moment—putting our disconnected members of arms and legs, head and torso back together. In a sense, when we break out of automatic pilot and we put our entire self back together into a state of wholeness.

Golfing is no exception to automatic pilot. Ideally, Mind Fitness will be a thread woven through everything we do on the golf course. It will be present in our pre-shot routine, present in the swing, and present in post-swing experience. It will also be present while walking and enjoying the natural beauty of the green grass beneath our feet. With practice these threads will be felt more frequently. Recalling that *any* activity can be one that engages Mind Fitness so long as we disengage from the Storytelling Mind and pay attention to our senses, there are countless opportunities to remember during the course of our day.

Remembering is good and we also need to guard against unrealistic expectations for our capacity to remember. Even after we have been practicing Mind Fitness for a while, we often can be swept up and away by the Storytelling Mind. If we can appreciate this as the nature of the mind, then we won't have to make distraction into a problem. In fact, distraction is just another opportunity for awareness. If, however, the old habit patterns of the mind are seen as signs of weakness, laziness, or stupidity, we are going make the distraction worse.

Mind Fitness practice is an invitation to keep weaving the threads of awareness.

6. Wi-Fi

The successful swing is grounded in *feel*. We want to cultivate a connection to this energy and can do so through Mind Fitness. The pro Eddie Loos gave some advice. He suggested using the walk down the fairway to maintain a close connection to the club about to be swung: "Feel the club head and let it swing you." The heft of the club can help to connect us to the *feel-image* (FI) of the swing.

Use the time between shots to cultivate this connection to the FI of the shot. As you walk down the fairway or walk from the fairway to the green, notice what is happening in the body. After you have grounded your attention in the present moment of the body, you can open to the FI of the next shot. This FI is a representation of what you would like to see happen. It can be very specific, accounting for the lie and the distance to your next destination. It can also be a general sense of a relaxed swing.

Let's pause for a moment and think about what it means to play relaxed because the term "relaxation" conjures many different meanings, some of which may not be helpful while playing golf. What I really mean is to get out of our own way and to allow the body and mind to do what they know how to do. We abandon the excess effort that can bias the swing. We "relax"—let go— into the swing and let it happen without interference. This is when we get our best results.

The relaxed FI feels fluid, unhurried, and connected to the target. When we bring the relaxed FI into awareness we are priming the motor areas of the brain for action and then providing a set of instructions. Relaxed awareness also establishes confidence in the next shot, as if we are moving toward the shot with poise.

The sport psychologist Shane Murphy captures the essence of FI when he describes learning to play golf: "For a long time, it seemed as if the golf swing would remain a series of disjointed parts, performed with great effort and no fluidity. But with repeated practice, I could stand over the ball and 'feel' the movements I needed to make to strike the ball cleanly; that moment marked a turning point in the development of my golf game. I had captured an *image* of what my swing should *feel* like and no longer had to rely on verbal reminders" (emphases added).

Research has shown that "golfers have improved their game when focusing on the motion of the club head in chip shots rather than the bend in the elbow or stiffness of the wrists." This external over internal focus approach emphasizes club movement over swing thoughts on the position of the arms. Arm position, as a swing thought, is a concept that can actually deter performance. We want to be able *feel* the swing, and the club path is integral to this movement. The movement of the club through the swing occurs in the dynamic present and connects us to our bodies.

The accuracy of the FI will increase the more we train the mind through Mind Fitness. The more intimate we become with our minds, the more accessible FI will become. When we *Wi-Fi—walk into feel-image*—we are tuning into our stored wisdom for hitting golf shots. Like Wi-Fi for the Internet, it is as if we are picking up the signals needed for the next shot. Mind Fitness can help us tune into these signals and use them to make the best shots that we can make.

7. You Can't Think Your Way Out of a Problem Thinking Got You into in the First Place

> Short of cardiac arrest (or a poisonous tick bite), nothing of mortal significance is likely to occur while one is whacking a small dimpled sphere across gentle green grass under a warm tropical sun. Only a miserably manic soul—and I'm not alone—would allow such a pleasantly inconsequential distraction as golf to be ruined by a scorecard. Yet every weekend, thousands of otherwise rational men and women are cursing, kicking at divots, and smashing expensive milled putters against the trunks of immovable hardwood trees. These players go home in toxic funk to inflict gloom upon their loved ones until the following Saturday, when they rush back to the golf course and do it all over again. Trying to be good at something isn't a bad idea. But, in the turbulent and random scroll of life, topping a tee shot is a meaningless if not downright comic occurrence. - Carl Hiaasen

If you resemble the men and women that Carl Hiaasen describes above, then what I call your "Strident Self" may be overly active. It is a fine thing to take the game of golf seriously but perilous to take ourselves so seriously. When we do, destructive emotions are bound to show up on the golf course.

Rick Reilly, in his very funny and illuminating book *Who's Your Caddy?,* describes the two years he spent caddying for, as he put it, "the great, near great, and reprobates of golf." He tried numerous times to get Tiger Woods to allow him to caddy. Each time the answer was no. Finally, Reilly pressed him for an explanation. Here it was: "I suck, I need good help." After reading that, I put the book down astonished. "Really?" Wow, so even the great have an active Strident Self, and this was before Tiger's epic scandal. Tiger can apparently use this harsh self-appraisal to keep himself motivated to become, perhaps, the greatest ever, but it would be hard to find a person, golfer or not, that would see this self-assessment as accurate.

The Strident Self is the Storytelling mind run amok. When it comes to golf, there is no shortage of things we can condemn ourselves over. We berate ourselves for unexpected and unwanted outcomes: topped balls, missed putts, hooks, slices, and dreaded shanks. Cows chew their food, swallow it into one of their stomachs and then regurgitate it and swallow again it into another stomach for more processing. This is an apt metaphor for the type of thinking that has come to be known as "rumination." We've essentially forgotten the metaphor. The mind chews events, feelings, and perceived and real outcomes again and again. Unlike the cows that are getting value from the rumination, we rarely do. It helps to think briefly about what went wrong with a shot but after that it's overkill. Mostly, rumination chronically activates our stress response system and we know that stress equals tension. We try to think ourselves out of a problem that thinking got us into in the first place. It's like trying to dig ourselves out of a hole while standing in the hole. The more we dig, the deeper in we get. It doesn't work. Stop digging!

Robert Allenby is a good case in point for how Mind Fitness can help you get beyond the Strident Self. Golf Magazine asked him, "You had fifteen top tens from 2007 to 2008. How did you jump-start your game?" Allenby talks about working with his "life coach": "What he does is remove all the crap, the things that you make up, the things that you worry about that aren't true. I've been working on the present instead of worrying about what I did two years ago or what could happen in the future. It's really helped my golf because it doesn't matter if I miss a putt. It doesn't matter if I hit it in the trees left—it's only a golf shot. In the past it's always been, "Oh, you idiot! What did you do that for?" That's been the biggest change in my game. I'm playing golf with complete freedom."

The Strident Self isn't limited to golf, of course. The once promising quarterback Vince Young was apparently suicidal and despondent after a poor performance. One of his former coaches at the University of Texas, requesting anonymity, said: "Nobody puts more pressure on himself. When things don't go well, Vince puts it on him. He is a perfectionist in his football. Things weigh on him. They weigh on him much more than the average person. You can't let him get in a dark hole that he can't come out of."

Richard Keefe, author of *On the Sweet Spot,* reminds us, "Constant attention to an external view of oneself is the core of human angst. If we could think of disastrous shots as one unfortunate possibility in a pleasant pastime, we would be better able to enjoy the challenge of the moment."

8. Beware the Fine Print

> Golf is the hardest game in the world. There's no way you can ever get it. Just when you think you do, the game jumps up and puts you in your place.—Ben Crenshaw

Awareness is only part of the story—the tip of the iceberg, if you will. At any given moment, we are being inundated with information and we can only give our attention to a small portion of what's actually happening. In order to deal with these massive amounts of information, the sensory organs use filters and so does the brain. The brain creates categories that help us figure out what we should be paying attention to. We apply these categories to every moment. For example, we have categories for the game of golf. One of these recognizes the features of the golf experience such that we can show up at a golf course we've never been to before and know how to proceed. We have a general category in our minds for "golf course" that includes subcategories for tee boxes, fairways, bunkers, and greens. We also carry around such categories for ourselves as golfers. These categories can combine to form a mental model, for instance, "I'm a choker, I always crack under pressure." This model is very different from, "I'm a good golfer, I enjoy the challenge of pressure." The differences in these models and their underlying assumption's is based on different personal histories—they each process information differently and can affect performance accordingly.

At the conscious—or near conscious—level, we bring agendas to every golf moment. The primary agenda is: "This is a 9-iron to the back of the green." The secondary agenda is: "I really need to stick this to get par here; if I bogey this hole, I'm really in trouble, and my round is going to hell." The primary agenda is practical and reality oriented. It is focused on the game and how it needs to be played. This is an adaptive and non-problematic use of the thinking-talking mind. Secondary agendas are usually not adaptive, in fact they can be downright irrational, especially when they confuse our golf score with our value as a human being. The secondary agenda is fueled by the Storytelling Mind—and perhaps even the Strident Self version of the Storytelling Mind. If we suffer on the golf course, secondary agendas are likely the cause.

The story of Mohini, the great white tiger, tells us something about the power of categories. She was kept at the National Zoo for many years in a 12' x 12' barred cage. A patron concerned with her plight endowed a natural habitat area for her so she could be free to roam. Unfortunately, instead of roaming free she paced a 12' x 12' patch into the grassy expanse that was now her home. We often live within the prison of our conditioning. The limits we have learned may not exist in the actual world.

Fortunately, we can give up our secondary agendas without sacrificing performance. This is how we can figure out, in part, what is primary and what is secondary. We can ask ourselves, "How do these thoughts serve my game?" Usually secondary agendas are not about how to golf but the *imagined* consequences of our golf results.

Managing the Storytelling Mind and its secondary agendas is a prime target of Mind Fitness. The more intimate we become with how our minds work, the more we can recognize and avoid the destructive influence of the Storytelling Mind and its secondary agendas.

Another concept that might be helpful is the notion of inclusion versus exclusion. The secondary agenda is very "exclusive." It attempts to exclude particular outcomes from happening and, by doing so, creates anxiety by forcing the mind to become protective—*I might not get what I want.* Letting go of the secondary agenda leads to an "inclusive" attitude—acceptance. Every sport psychologist preaches the value of acceptance but it often takes more than exhortation to become accepting. We make our shot and then we must then accept the results and move on. When the shot goes bad we ask ourselves—*what did I learn here?*—and integrate that bit of information for future shots. This feedback process is very different from insisting that things should be a particular way and getting emotional—

frustrated, angry, disheartened—when they don't go as planned. If you find yourself having these types of feelings on the course, your secondary agendas are running the show.

One note of caution. As we engage in Mind Fitness training and begin to see results from our practice, the Storytelling Mind will start to generate secondary agendas about this progress, just as it makes up secondary agendas about our progress—or lack thereof—in golf. Watch out for these secondary agendas. We can acknowledge progress without needing to set new and unreasonable standards for ourselves. Be patient. Progress, while generally moving in an upward direction, will not move in a perfectly straight line. Just as our game can hit impasses and plateaus, our capacity for concentration and dealing with secondary agendas can get stuck as well. Keep practicing and you are bound to be successful.

9. Fierce Attention

> The athlete who can focus on the task at hand avoids distraction and enjoys the greatest possibility of success.—Clark Perry

The golf swing has been described as "controlled violence." Striking a small plastic ball with enough force to send it perhaps over 300 yards is not a gentle activity. Fierce Attention is the mind's version of controlled violence. We stalk the golf ball as a tiger stalks its prey. The tiger is stealth and waits until the right moment to pounce. It does not roar and make a fuss beforehand. It strikes not with brutality but with elegance. The predatory cat is pure enjoyment. It is supple, nimble, and focused. It is ferocious and goal oriented. By being so focused, there is no separation from itself and its goal. It is the goal, it is the path, it is the execution. The stalking cat is incapable of getting "emotional" when it misses its prey. She can't blame herself and bemoan her fate. Even if she could, she'd miss the next opportunity to pounce and catch her prey. Missing is no big deal because other opportunities are coming. Like the tiger, nothing should come between you and your swing—especially thoughts. The tiger approaches with an intensity of focus and so should you. While fierce attention comes naturally for the tiger, we need to train it through Mind Fitness. If we want our shots to be elegant violence instead of brute force, we'll need to learn from the tiger.

When you think of the focused mind, do you conjure images of tranquility? Why can't it also be ferocious? It can be when we define concentration as an "awareness that we use in doing whatever is before us, being both sharp and relaxed. When we are both attentive and matter-of-fact, we do not tire easily, because we feel refreshed and renewed through a smooth engagement of our awareness."

Mind Fitness practice does not just happen when we formally set out to do mind training exercises. Life provides many opportunities to pay attention in this deliberate way. In fact, the larger purpose of formal practice is to maximize the likelihood that Mind Fitness will "spill over" into life general.

The consequences of attention that is not fierce can be regrettable. Take the case of the Shane Bertsch. He lost his Tour card for 2009 through an unfortunate combination of misunderstanding and impaired performance. Approaching the final Tour event—The Children's Miracle Network Classic at Walt Disney World—he was under the mistaken impression that due to a medical extension in 2007 his previous winnings would exempt him until 2009. Just prior to the event, he discovered this impression was false. He was 124th on the money list going into the tournament. He missed the cut by two strokes and then lost his tour card by one stroke when Martin Laird sunk a putt from 8 feet on the final hole. Bertsch tells us of his confused and beleaguered mental state, "I couldn't even play. I don't know that I've ever played under that much pressure. I couldn't pull the trigger I was so nervous. I had so many thoughts running through my head that how could this be happening to me?" And his game would attest to this; he missed six putts inside of 8 feet.

Unfortunately for Bertsch, he was not able to keep his focus on the present, which might have allowed him to perform adequately enough to retain his card. Instead, his anxiety became overwhelming and destroyed his concentration. He was not able to maintain fierce attention to the task at hand. His mind was undisciplined. Certainly, the news revealed to him just prior to the event was compelling but not relevant to playing *that* event. His mind was stuck in the implications of that news. Awash in confusion, regret, and worry, he underperformed. Had he made the cut, he would have retained his card. When we step on the course and stand over the ball it behooves us for the fews seconds surrounding the shot to be fiercely concentrated, paying attention to what is most relevant in the moment and only that. Fortunately for the recreational player, the consequences of an attention lapse don't typically carry as much gravity as Shane Bertsch's situation. Fierce Attention can help us to play our best. It won't guarantee that you "keep your card," but it will guarantee that you give it your best shot.

NEUROSCIENCE

This section presents cutting edge research from the neurosciences and psychology. Recent advances in brain imaging have led to fascinating discoveries about how the brain works and provide us with important clues on how to improve our golf game. We'll also discover what's going on in the brain when we're playing well and when we are playing poorly.

10. Going Unconscious

The philosopher Alfred North Whitehead said: "Civilization advances by extending the number of important operations which we can perform without thinking about them." This insight can be applied to golf: *Your game will improve to the extent that you can perform the skills of golf without thinking about them.*

Learning is a self-conscious process and mastery is an unconscious one. Our ancestors needed to adapt to a changing, unpredictable, potentially dangerous world of experiences and they accomplished that by being especially sensitive to new information. We share that legacy; it's in our DNA. Once information is no longer new, the brain rotates it into unconscious automatic processing thus freeing conscious attention to notice other novel things because novel may be danger, novel may be opportunity. When we learning a skill, it migrates from the front of the brain to the middle of the brain—from the frontal cortex to the motor and somatosensory parts of the brain.

If you drag your finger across the top of your head, ear-to-ear, you will be tracing the motor and somatosensory areas. The motor area allocates its real estate to those activities we use the most. For instance, it gives large parcels of "land" to our fingers and our tongue—just think of the complex movements you can make with your tongue! — and relatively little to our torso, unless, of course, you are a belly dancer. If you become a concert pianist, finger real estate grows further still. As we practice golf, we are telling the brain to allocate real estate resources to support this activity. The more we play, the more we will have neurons—brain nerve cells—devoted to the movements that make the golf swing. Practice moves us from having to "talk" through the shot self-consciously, to being able to make the swing without conscious thought—purely through image and feel. Of course, that doesn't prevent us from talking to ourselves through a golf shot but it's no longer necessary. A research study has found that professional pianists show a pattern of brain activation where the "talk" parts of the brain are quiet—the frontal lobes. These frontal parts of the brain would be involved in self-conscious monitoring of the *initiation* of action. This monitoring is absent for the expert musicians. Instead, their movements appear to be regulated by the unconscious parts of the brain, such as the motor area and the cerebellum (at the back and bottom of the brain).

Self-consciousness explains much of why novices are, well, novices. "Athletes who need to focus a large percentage of their [conscious] energy on the primary task often exhibit 'tunnel vision' in regard to secondary tasks that require a broad band of attention. As a consequence, errors often occur." In other words, the novice is too preoccupied with swing thoughts to give attention to the subtle factors that can lead to sticking an approach shot next to the pin and rolling a putt in from yards away. They can't concentrate the manner an expert can concentrate due to the way the brain is activated.

We can see unconscious processes in action by undermining them with self-consciousness. There is the fable of the centipede who was asked how he managed to walk with all those legs. He could no longer walk after he thought about it. Many things we do are done unconsciously, such as signing your name, walking, and breathing. Try to do these activities deliberately and you'll notice a self-conscious disruption.

We get beyond self-consciousness through practice. Mastery allows us to access information deep in the brain that would not otherwise be available. At times, even without mastery, we get "gifts" from our unconscious, such as the one described here by Richard Keefe: "An elevated certainty about future events, such as a prescient image of making a putt, may come from an increase in information suddenly available to us that we did not know we possessed. We see the line perfectly, and develop a certainty that we know exactly what the roll will be like, what stroke and speed are required. We have accessed more information than usual, and a part of our brain knows that."

11. 100:1

> During any given second, we consciously process only sixteen of the eleven million bits of information our senses pass on to our brains.—Tor Norretranders

If we understand a little bit more about how consciousness works, we can have a deeper appreciation for how flimsy, fragile, and fickle it can be. With this appreciation in hand, we'll be more motivated to train attention so we can get more than the sixteen bits that are typically available.

The first issue to consider is that the world is not as it appears. We only see what our eyes can see; we only hear what our ears can hear. This is a hardware issue—the limits of our eyes, ears, and other sensory organs. Unlike dogs we cannot hear sounds above 20,000 hertz and unlike bats we cannot see light in the infrared band of the electromagnetic light spectrum. Reality, then, is only *our* human reality.

Second, our senses have to reduce the overabundance of data they receive. Our eyes, for instance, filter out 99 percent of the available information before sending it to the brain. This one per cent becomes what we see. We appear to be much more conscious than we actually are. This is a software issue—how we process the limited amount of information we have access to. We are only aware of a sliver of a sliver.

There have been some fascinating studies on a concept called *inattentional blindness* that demonstrate the power of this selective process. In these studies, subjects watched a video of a group of six people, three white shirts and three black shirts, each group throwing a basketball back and forth. The experimental subject is asked to count the number of times the ball is thrown by either the black or the white shirts thus engaging attention on a counting task. While this is happening a person in a gorilla suit walks into the picture frame, beats its chest, and exits stage left. Incredibly, only 50 percent of the subjects noticed the gorilla. Obviously, every subject's eyes "saw" the gorilla—their eyes and brains processed the information—yet, many did not "see" the gorilla. It did not enter attention.

Finally, this sliver is biased by what we've learned in the past, what we expect to be happening now, and a host of other factors, including our intentions. For instance, in a sense as "objective" as vision, only 20 percent of our visual information comes from the retina and, astoundingly, the rest comes from areas of the brain associated with memory. In this way, vision can be as much as 90 percent "best-guess" brain perception. If memory can affect raw perception, imagine what it could do to performance on a hole we've had recent trouble with or a club that has not been behaving. If consciousness is a limited resource—and it is those skimpy sixteen out of eleven million bits—our assumptions will bias us towards what we believe, whether we are aware of these beliefs or not.

What we pay attention to will also be determined by what is deemed relevant. When we play golf, mental categories will be active. When we get to a "difficult" hole, we activate a category that includes beliefs based on past performance. Since the brain (processing capacity) and mind (selection based on relevance) constructs our experience of the world, we can work to alter these constructions. If we "believe" that we might fail, the brain—as if by magic—arranges that result. If we can set that belief aside, we can choose another outcome.

12. Amy G. Dala

As we have established, our working definition for concentration is paying full attention to whatever we deem to be *most* relevant in the moment. How do we determine what is most relevant? This can be a rational, cognitive process, but in most cases the allocation of scarce attention resources needs to be authorized by the emotional brain. The problem with this is that our emotional brain—and every other part of our brain—evolved a long time ago—50,000 to 100,000 years ago. It did not evolve to play golf or to manage most of the challenges of modern life such as technology, crowds, and traffic. We thus live with a mismatch between the environment our brains evolved within and the environment they function in today. This mismatch is the source of most of our stress.

The threats our ancestors faced in that environment long ago were mostly physical: predators, starvation, extreme temperatures, and other humans. The threats from other humans were social with physical consequences: "Is this other person friend or foe?" "Is he going to beat me up and steal my food and water?" Over the millennia as language developed and human groups became more complex, what might be perceived as threatening has also changed. We live in a situation now where events on a golf course can activate the protective functions of that old brain. There has been a migration from actual physical threats to threats to our self-image. These threats are more theoretical than actual because usually what is being threatened is an idea, belief, expectation, or rule. It's our pride on the line, not our life. Since we no longer have to fight for our survival, the brain is free to protect the ego.

An important component of the emotional brain is a structure called the amygdala. The amygdala's job is to figure out what we should be paying attention to. Threats get first dibs. Opportunities come next. It also helps us to act "on what we unconsciously know to be true, even if we are not aware that it is right."

The emotional brain helps us to figure out what is relevant in any given moment. Remember that novelty is key because new information may be about a threat or an opportunity. *Was that a tiger that just entered my field of vision? Is that a source of water over there?* The emotional brain works rapidly and unconsciously to mobilize a response to this potential danger.

If we look at a snapshot of the brain in the midst of emotional activation, the colors in the threat response system would show red, indicating a lot of metabolism in that region. Once the danger has been recognized and a response authorized, the stress response system kicks in and takes action. The unfortunate state of affairs is that this activity can occur standing over a birdie putt just as it would if a tiger had been spotted—and I mean an actual Bengal tiger: *Panthera tigris tigris.* However, professional golfers have been known to experience a similar stress response upon seeing the other Tiger, too, species: *Panthera Woods.* What we don't want to be relevant in the exact moment of a golf swing is self-image protection. The golf swing is too fragile to withstand that sort of ego strain; it needs all the brain resources we can muster.

13. Mirror, Mirror on the Wall

Golf is usually a social activity. Like processing sensory perception, the brain processes social perception. Part of the brain's social architecture is *resonance circuits* that help us to navigate through the social world. One of the primary functions of resonance circuits is to figure out the intentions of others. It accomplishes this feat through the use of *mirror neurons.* These mirror neurons and resonance circuits attempt to replicate internally what we see others doing. In this way, we can try to figure out what they are doing and what their intentions are. "Is this a friendly action and should I approach?" Or, "Is this an unfriendly action and should I avoid?" By replicating the experience of the other, we can protect ourselves or make connections and by mirroring and resonating we also have the capacity for empathy.

Mirror neurons may explain a curious phenomenon that happens on the course. Have you ever noticed that your shot may follow the exact path of the previous player's shot? If that shot goes right, your shot goes right, perhaps landing a few feet away from that first ball. This is uncanny! Perhaps. It is more comprehensible when you think about mirror neurons. If you watch the player in front of you swing, your brain creates a *feeling image* of that shot in an attempt to understand what it is seeing. The brain attempts to replicate in ourselves what it sees in the other person. The brain is doing its job according to how the brain evolved eons ago. Unless your mind creates a clear and vivid image of the shot *you* want to make, your swing may operate on the "instructions" of the other person's swing. Because of mirror neurons we need to overwrite the image of the last shot before executing our next shot.

One suggestion is not to look at the shots of others, unless they are making an exquisite swing that you wish to emulate. Turn your head!

14. See the Shot; Be the Shot

> When you are playing your best, you look down at the ball on the tee and you see the fairway and the spot out there where your shot's going to land. It's almost like looking at those score cards that have a map of each hole, with the play of the hole marked in dotted lines. What you see is the dotted line. Of course, if you're playing bad, what you see are the woods and the traps, Marlboro Country, and more often than not, if that's

what you're thinking, that's where your shot is going to end up.—Dave Marr

Imagery is used by a vast majority of athletes. Imagery is used to prepare for competition, deal with errors in technique, learn new skills, and relax. It's a potent tool in sport psychology and the cornerstone technique emerging from this field. It is a multisensory experience that sees the shot and also hears it and most importantly feels it. Kinesthetic imagery—the imagined feeling of movement—is the cornerstone imagery tool. As discussed above, Mind Fitness connects us directly to the feeling-image (FI) of the shot. Thus, Mind Fitness is an excellent way to develop access to the FI of playing golf well.

Visualization works so well because, at some level, our brains cannot tell the difference between what is real and what is imagined. When we picture a golf shot, a brain scan would reveal activity in the visual cortex, even though our eyes see nothing. I jokingly tell my students that "the mind is smart, and the brain is dumb." (But that is a conceit because there are many situations—like believing cognitive distortions where the mind appears to be dumb). The brain is an information processor that cannot tell the difference between what is real and what is imagined—just think of how we can get anxious, aroused, or elated purely through memory or reading a thriller. When we imagine ourselves engaging in an activity as if we are doing it, the same parts of the brain—motor cortex, the prefrontal cortex, and the cerebellum—that would be active during the actual activity are engaged. And this activity is not limited to the brain. Intensive imagination may activate the muscle groups involved in the imagined activity, such as the legs or arms.

We become skilled at activities through repetition. Each repetition develops a motor plan in the brain. This plan contains the neural circuits involved in executing the action. The more these are practiced the more automatic and unconscious they become. Imagery can activate these motor plans before the desired action, thus priming brain and body for action. In other words, visualizing your swing in imagination actually helps you to prepare to make that swing. Jack Nicklaus was reported to have said that he "wouldn't swing the club until he was able to see the shot he wanted to hit."

Gold medalist bobsledder Gustav Weder used elaborate visualization to great success in the Lillehammer Olympic Games. He took photographs of the course and laid them out on his living room floor. Each day, he would imagine going through the course in preparation for the event. This is also good strategy for any golfer. During a practice round of a tournament, let's say, take mental pictures from the course and then practice playing around the course in your imagination. See and feel each shot as you would like it to happen. Make the imagery as rich as possible, including the sounds and smells you noticed, and—again—the feeling of each shot as you imagine it. One advantage of having a home course is familiarity and the richer, more detailed images can be created. Playing the course in imagination could be just as valuable as actually playing! One compelling story illustrates this point. An American Colonel was imprisoned in a POW camp for several years. He coped, in part, by imagining a round of golf every day. Upon his return from captivity he shot a round at par after not having picked up a club in years.

Imagery can help us, as already discussed, prepare for action, and it can also help to motivate us towards that action, providing inspiration, confidence, and even joy. Imagery gives marching orders to the brain. It helps us to select the direction and intensity of effort. The image of the perfectly struck shot is also pleasant and thereby reinforcing. We can imagine ourselves improving, overcoming obstacles, and attaining desired skills or we can imagine ourselves vanquishing our opponent in match play. In addition to motivation and confidence, imagery can also help us to concentrate. Remembering that concentration is paying attention to whatever is deemed most relevant in the moment, imagery can help us to focus on the relevant details, especially the feeling of the swing. Such concentration helps us to access important information at crucial times that it may be needed, like staying composed in a pressure-packed situation .

One study found that golfers learning to putt did better when practice was accompanied by imagery. Interestingly, these young putters also saw improvement from just swinging their putters without striking a ball, as this motion of "putting to nowhere" develops the feeling-image of the swing.

Making the shot in imagination helps the brain to aim at the target because it not only sees the target with the eyes but goes to the target in the mind's eye. This process of outer and inner looking helps us to collect all the information we need to make our best shot. Most of this information is processed unconsciously.

The more clear and vivid the image, the more preparation that occurs. Many players "see" a path to their shot. This may take the form of a dotted line or colored line. Recently the Golf Channel implemented a new technology that shows the line of a putt on the screen. The viewer can then watch if the ball rolls along that line and, if so, drop in. If we can generate such a line in our mind's eye of imagination, it should increase the likelihood of that putt going in. This is not wishful thinking on our part—it's brain and body preparation.

Remember that the brain is "dumb"; if we use imagination incorrectly we can give ourselves the wrong "instructions" and wind up in "Marlboro Country." If your imagined swing or stroke is faulty, the real shot will follow that flawed path. Images can also undermine confidence if they are distorted. I made varsity track throwing the discus in my sophomore year of high school. The big man on campus was a guy named Jon. He was huge and held the record for the shot put. I looked "up" to him. One day, however, I was standing next to him and realized that I was as big as he was! It was only in my imagination that he was huge and daunting. This realization and correction of the image gave me the confidence to go on to break his record in my junior year. If you find yourself intimidated, check the accuracy of the underlying image. Remind yourself that you're "bigger" than the challenge.

George Plimpton presents a compelling example of how not to use imagination. He describes the vivid mind of pro golfer Clayton Heafner. He would: "Think of the indignities to which the golf course would subject him—the putts missed because of worm holes, the unraked sand traps, the bad lies in the sun-baked fairways; in his mind he would hear the clout of balls hitting tree trunks—such a variety of disturbing images and sound that sometimes when he'd get to the door of the headquarters room[...]he'd call out to them: 'Your golf course is a goddam pasture!' And then he would leave. His mind created an imaginary world of persecution."

Like any other attribute, people vary in their ability to evoke vivid and controllable images. Imagination, as with attention, is like a muscle and can be developed through practice. Imagination fitness is a key component of Mind Fitness. If imagery is challenging for you it is a skill that can be developed using the imagery exercises in the Appendix.

15. 10,000 Hours or 10 Years, Whichever Comes First

> I had a few good holes, which is all that any dumbass needs to fool himself into thinking he's got talent.—Carl Hiaasen

At the same time, we underestimate and overestimate the complexity of the golf swing. We underestimate the intricate patterns of muscle control and coordination it requires. We overestimate the effort we need to make and then try too hard. Expertise will develop with repetition and at the moment of each swing we must allow the body to do what it knows how to do in that moment. However, unless you've logged approximately 10,000 hours of play and practice making that swing over the course of 10 years, you have unlikely reached expert status. Harvey Penick reminds us, "Ben (Hogan) practiced thousands of hours perfecting his swing."

Ian Poulter got admonished for standing in the same spot for six hours on the practice putting green in advance of the 2008 Open Championship in Royal Birkdale. Apparently, he wore brown spots in the carpet. Can you imagine spending six hours taking practice putts from the same place? If not, that's probably why none of us came in second at the British Open.

10,000 are a lot of hours. If playing golf were your full-time job, you'd reach 10,000 in about five years, say a day at the office consists of eighteen holes and four hours of practice. Think about it this way. If a round of golf takes 4 hours, it would require 2,500 rounds of golf to attain 10,000 hours. But this is only time playing golf, which certainly is not 10,000 hours swinging the club. And since golf is comprised of several different activities, the requirements grow. Do we have 10,000 hours hitting our driver? Do we have 10,000 hours hitting irons? Do we have 10,000 hours hitting bunker shots? Do we have 10,000 hours hitting wedges? Do we have 10,000 hours putting?—better make that 20,000! If you are anything but a touring professional, the answer to these queries will almost certainly be no. Yet, when we make a poor shot we bring a groundless set of expectations about the level of our expertise to judge that shot: We are not experts and should not judge ourselves as such.

The hours are one consideration; the quality and duration of practice are others. These 10,000 hours ideally occur over the span of ten years. This is known as the "10-year rule." This rule states that "no person can make creative contributions to a particular domain without first devoting a full decade to the mastery of the necessary knowledge and skills." Of course, 10,000 of bad practice will make you an expert in bad golfing. Hours spent learning with experts will make the most of those practice hours.

The incredible variability in hitting golf shots—especially for novices and intermediates makes us think that we are—or can be—much more expert than we are. Occasionally, we all hit beautiful shots. However, unreasonable expectations arise when these beautiful shots become the reference standard for all future shots. Since they cannot yet be produced reliably, frustration arises. I have yet to log my 2,500 rounds, let alone all the hours on the different aspects of my game. This awareness is a soothing balm after a poor shot. I must remind myself that I am a neophyte and, while I can sometimes play with brilliance, I cannot sustain this level of play dependably. Improvement is also—frustratingly and misleadingly—not linear. I've got to be in it for the long haul. Occasional attention to our game is not enough to overcome the variance. Few can claim the requisite hours to achieve "expert" status. Can the rest of us relax into this knowledge?

It takes many hours to program the brain to play golf unconsciously. "The beginning player takes forever over the ball because he is still trying to figure out what to do. The beginner's mind is a jumble of conflicting motor programs. The tour player just sits back and lets it go." This is also why introducing a change to your swing, even at the professional level, can impair performance temporarily. A change forces the brain to be conscious of the new approach and the mind may be inundated with swing thoughts and the motor cortex has yet to ingrain the change.

Patience is a good antidote to the frustrations that arise from being a beginner. Dedication to practice is another. Inborn talent alone does not make a great golfer, practice does. Even experts can substantially improve their performance with dedicated efforts. No one is exempt from this. Successful players like Jason Dufner and Tiger are known for the ferocity of their practice. Good practice emphasizes the *process* of golf. When we can embrace, enjoy, and engage with practice, we build the foundation of our expertise. While we may not reach 10,000 hours any time soon, each practice session and round played contributes to our development as a player.

16. Tiger's Tibia

Tiger Woods won the 2008 U.S. Open six weeks after knee surgery, with two stress fractures in his tibia. After the third round, during which he showed obvious pain, yet eagled two holes on the back nine, he said: "But if pain hits, pain hits. So be it. It's just pain." He almost won again at the 2013 Barclay's when he fell to his knees in back pain on the par 5 13th. He hooked that shot into the water and managed to save par. He almost forced a playoff when he birdied 16 and 17 and left a 30-foot put one revolution short on the edge of the cup at 18. Most of us would have crawled off the course defeated after a back spasm of that magnitude.

Tiger makes an important distinction between pain and suffering. He accepts the pain, makes room for it in his current experience, and does not allow it to interfere with his performance. He is not identifying with the pain or elaborating it into a story of woe. He is coping with it. By doing so, he pulled off one of the most remarkable feats in the history of sport by winning in 2008 U.S. Open after a full round playoff over Rocco Mediate. It's so easy to take a situation of pain or setback and make it into a story: "Why is this happening to me?" We let even minor discomforts get in our way of enjoying life and playing golf effectively.

Suffering and pain are not synonymous. Tiger was in pain yet he was not suffering—nor was his performance. Suffering arises out of wishing something wasn't happening and fighting against it—*resisting it*— and we can use this helpful formula: suffering = pain x resistance. When we resist what is present, we create tension. We squander precious mental resources to maintain this resistance. It takes energy to fight with pain. It takes attention bandwidth to complain about it, to feel victimized by it. Most of suffering is not caused by the intensity, duration or variety of pain. When we resist the pain, we multiply the experience of suffering. For example, if someone has ten units of physical pain, and ten units of mental pain and ten units of emotional pain the result is not 30 (10 + 10 +10) but 1,000 units of suffering (10 x

10 x 10). A fit mind that doesn't resist—that accepts—stops the suffering from multiplying.

Dividing and conquering is a Mind Fitness strategy. If we can bring a concentrated mind that does not narrate each component of the pain or misfortune, then we just have the 30 units of pain uncompounded into further suffering. This is equanimity in action. Equanimity is the degree to which we do not push and pull—resist—on our senses, perceptions, and experiences. When things are seen "clearly"—that is, with sensory clarity—they don't get compounded.

"Pain" is the conceptual label the brain applies to certain patterns of sensation, in other words, the firing of pain neurons. Understanding and responding to pain is highly adaptive and helps us to cope with illness and injury. It tells us, for example, we have cut or burned ourselves and directs attention to healing the tissue damage. The brain brings the message home with feeling: pain hurts. Its unpleasantness gets our attention and motivates action.

Tiger interpreted his pain as "just pain." That is, he did not see it as a problem requiring further intervention and elaboration. He did not generate a drama about the pain in which he played the starring role. He didn't bemoan the fact of his knee and how it might impair his chances at the Open. He didn't complain, "Why me?" Instead, he opened his attention to include the sensations of pain. He did not resist by creating an opposition between his intention to play golf and the experience of pain. It became a part of his landscape in the present moment. He winced and limped *after* executing his best shot and not before.

How often do we have to deal with some ache or pain? How often do we have to deal with bothersome conditions in the body such as fatigue, hunger, and thirst? How often do we create opposition to these conditions? The next time any currently unchangeable bothersome conditions arise see if you can open attention to include these in the landscape of your present moment. Expand the definition of yourself to be inclusive rather than exclusive. Don't make the pain or discomfort into a "problem" that needs a solution and don't waste vital attention and energy trying to solve a problem that can't be solved. Allow it to be there and go about executing your best shot. Of course, if you are actually injured—stop playing or modify your swing as needed. It's important to distinguish pain that contains important information from pain that does not. Unfortunately for Tiger, his heroics ignored important information that the pain he was experiencing might be leading to harm. He played against medical advice knowing he had the stress fractures. After his Open victory, he was done for the 2008 season requiring major reconstructive knee surgery.

Get to know your body intimately. The Body Scan practice (see the Appendix) does this for you. It familiarizes you with the entire body as it changes moment by moment. The Body Scan can help you to realize the body is comprised of dynamic energy. More important than what is happening in any given moment is how we relate to what is happening. This relationship can be one of acceptance or resistance. Resistance leads to suffering. Acceptance leads to peace.

17. Cool-Mad

Have you ever wondered why we have feelings at all? What is their purpose and function? To figure this out, it can helpful to make a distinction between emotions and feelings, although the terms are often used interchangeably. An emotion, especially the negative ones like anger or fear, is more of a reaction—a full-blown episode containing intense feelings, physiological arousal, and a temporary inability to function properly. Emotions arise as coping responses in situations where our ability to handle what's happening has been outstripped by the circumstances we are facing. Emotions are "expensive" in terms of energy, time, and disruption of function. Feelings, in contrast, are the background of awareness. They are always present and informing our experience whether pleasant or unpleasant. Feelings are always part of an emotional reaction, but they are not in and of themselves "emotions." This leads to the potentially confusing situation where all emotions contain feelings but not all feelings are emotions. Feelings help us to figure out the world. Before we had language and supermarkets, feelings helped us to move towards the things that would be good for us, such as healthful foods and sex, and away from things that would be bad for us, such as toxic foods and predators. To be in the right balance with emotions and feelings is to be, as Sam Snead called, "cool-mad." We need the energy of feeling but must keep it from becoming a disruptive emotion.

On the golf course, it is fair to say that we want to eliminate emotions altogether while increasing our access to feelings. Mind Fitness increases our attunement to feelings arising in the body, both as physical sensations and the feeling flavors they have. Just as children learn to outgrow temper tantrums as they develop more sophisticated cognitive and motor capacities to act in the world, we golfers should also try to outgrow emotions on the links. We can do this in the same developmental fashion as children: by increasing our cognitive and motor skills.

Another way to think of the feeling system is top-down versus bottom-up processing. In top-down processing, we frame experience with an idea that moves down into the body. For example, a false belief that you have just been exposed to poison ivy leads to psychosomatic itching—the "mind" activates the "body." In bottom-up processing the direction is reversed—an itching in the body leads to the realization that "that must have been poison ivy where I was hunting for my ball." The "body" in this case activates the "mind." We want to be oriented bottom-up when playing golf rather than top-down, especially when top-down undermines confidence. For instance, if you are thinking, "I can never putt this green," this belief will create tension in the body that may actually help to confirm your belief. Instead, if you are focused on relaxed feelings in your body and your feeling-image for the swing (bottom-up), you are more likely to execute the shot that you want.

The FIT mind is bottom-up. It helps us to tap into the vast wisdom of the feeling body and to use this body to play in a focused and relaxed manner.

SPORT PSYCHOLOGY

There is a science to sport. Much of what we know from psychology can help athletes to perform at their best. Building on the foundation of mind training we've developed in the first two sections, we'll look at how to transform adversity into advantage, best practices, and skill.

18. Perfectomy

> *No person, athlete or not, can do things perfectly the first time and every time.—Mitch Abrams and Bruce Hale*

Aspiring to be the best is a noble goal. *Demanding* that we be perfect is a pitfall that can block the path to being your best. Of course, perfection in golf is more of an aspiration than reality. No one has shot the perfect round: 54. Expecting perfection is unrealistic. The game of golf consists of thousands of variables and conditions, many of which are not under our direct control. Yet, we may unreasonably insist upon perfection. Our force of will cannot trump the laws of physics, although sometimes it might feel as if it should. When we insist on the unreasonable, we set ourselves up for frustration. What we tell ourselves seems to be most responsible for this pressure for perfection and it's a safe bet that if we're putting all these expectations on ourselves it's hard to accept when things don't go according to plan.

Mind Fitness is like a lobotomy for perfectionism—a "perfectomy" if you will. One of the benefits of Mind Fitness training is noticing how we have unrealistic standards of perfection and, at the same time, not buying into them. To understand perfectionism, we must know what our implicit rules are—the thoughts that guide our beliefs. To find out what the rules are, we must know our minds and what we tell ourselves. This discovery applies to the obvious rules—thoughts that circulate through our conscious mind—as well as the not so obvious thoughts, beliefs, and stories that may be operating just outside of conscious awareness. These unconscious thoughts form our "rule book." And unlike the USGA Rule Book, ours may be arbitrary, capricious, and strident. We must look within ourselves and go beneath the surface to see what's there. To go "low" in the mind requires clearing away all the distractions at the surface—those loud and noisy thoughts. Once these are cleared, we can "hear" our opinions about ourselves, others, and the world. There are beliefs: "I am a good person" or "I am inadequate"; there are expectations: "I should be a scratch player by now"; there are condemnations: "If I don't play the way I *should* play, then there is something wrong with me"; and there are assumptions: "Golf isn't all that difficult; just look how easy the pros make it seem." These beliefs, expectations, condemnations, and assumptions comprise our mental programming—the rulebook—that will determine how we react to the situations we encounter. If we change the programming, we can change the reactions.

Perfectionism makes us vulnerable to feeling bad whenever a rule is broken. If we work to revise these rules to preferences—or even better to get rid of them altogether—then there are fewer situations that can provoke us into anger, disappointment, and frustration. Relaxing the rules gives our nervous system a break since every reaction is accompanied by a stress response. It also helps us to be more engaged and more satisfied with what is happening, including playing our game. The successful Perfectomy creates an open space of pleasure, relaxation, and freedom. Within this space we can have poor shots, holes, and rounds without losing our composure; we can play imperfectly and still enjoy playing.

Frustration, boredom, restlessness, and impatience may also point to perfectionism. Whenever these feelings are active in your experience, consult your rulebook.

Better managing perfectionism is not an invitation to mediocrity; we can still work to improve and learn from any mistakes. The difference is when something unwanted happens we look at that shot with interest. "What did that missed putt just tell me?" "Oh, I steered that one; what can I do next time to avoid this?" We have identified a problem and derived some actionable feedback that can be incorporated to improve our game. This can be a refreshing alternative to self-condemnation for missing a three-foot putt and wanting to bury that putter in the green or, better yet, throw it in the pond.

Underlying perfectionism is a resistance to being ordinary. To be perfect is to be special and at some level we all want to be special. However, especially in the realm of golf, we are destined to be ordinary—if we are lucky! Psychologist Polly Young-Eisendrath suggests that "learning the difference between self-blame and responsibility awakens our humility and brings into focus our sense of being ordinary." We can take responsibility for our actions without having to punish ourselves. This is what a Perfectomy can provide. The benefits of this will extend beyond our golf game. The perfectionist at golf will be a perfectionist in other areas of life. However, demanding perfection and meting out punishment for shortfalls can lead to a lot of mental anguish. If we can embrace being ordinary in a responsible way, we can find a way out of this trap.

19. The Inner Light

> Even beginners hit one of these sweet-spot shots now and then. The rush of thrill and excitement resulting from it is what inspires learners to want to get better, so they can have this wondrous feeling again.—Harvey Penick

Intrinsic motivation is motivation by process—the pleasure that comes from the process of playing. Recall the joy of a shot hit on the sweet spot. Extrinsic motivation is motivation by outcome—low scores, victories, and preventing losses. Shifting an intrinsically motivated athlete to extrinsic motivation can diminish performance. Have you seen this with your swing? If you make a natural swing and hit the ball well, extrinsic orientation wants more distance (outcome) rather than more purity of the swing (process). Extrinsic orientation—and the striving effort that it recruits—actually interfere with the natural swing. Research in sport psychology has consistently found that intrinsic feelings are the most potent motivators.

The story of Mr. Coyne speaks to the value of intrinsic motivation. Coyne, a 6-handicap, had "lost his swing." After having been beaten badly by a double-digit handicapper without giving strokes, he decided to quit the game. He went into the caddy shack and let the young caddies have the pick of his clubs: the mid-iron, the brassie, niblick, spoon, cleek, mashie, jigger, and the heavy mid-iron. He went home determined to give up this foul game. He imagined his wife's triumphant reception of this news, for she would no longer be a golf "widow." As it turns out, she was not home, which left Mr. Coyne by himself. Somehow, he "found" an old rusted mid-iron in a closet and a ball in his son's room. It's not hard to imagine what happened next; in the solitary pleasure of his back yard he once again found his swing. He had gotten caught up in extrinsic motivation—his identity as low-handicapper. When his game became elusive, his frustration was in direct proportion to poor outcomes. Rediscovering the joy of his swing saved him. Fortunately for him, his clubs were saved by the savvy locker room attendant who, knowing no man could quit golf, bought Mr. Coyne's clubs back from the caddies.

What motivates your golf game? Why do you play golf? What are you seeking? Are you playing golf to become a more complete human being? Are you playing golf to develop your relationship between body and mind? If so, your motivation is intrinsic. Are you playing to reach a number, to win your club championship and garner the parking spot that goes with that honor? If the score on the scorecard or the numerals on your handicap index are what move you, your motivation is extrinsic. Of course, it is fine to have goals for your game. These can be good targets to aim at. However, when your motivation is only or predominately these goals, you set yourself up for frustration.

20. Please Leave Your Ego, With Your Shoes, At the Door

> Everything is perfect and there is always room for improvement.—Shunryu Suzuki

When Sam Snead said, "forget your opponents; always play against par," he was advocating for task-mastery over an ego-orientation. Ego-orientation is a focus on winning and protecting our self-image as a golfer. Ego-orientation makes us vulnerable to perfectionism and its destructive effects. Of course, we can have both task- and ego-orientations, and it is impossible to remove all ego-oriented aspirations from our game. The ego-orientation needs to be managed with care, lest it get out of control and damage our game in both subtle and obvious ways.

Task-orientation leads to a kind of continuous quality improvement (CQI). CQI is a goal for corporations and one that can serve our golf game as well. The task-oriented golfer recognizes that "everything is perfect and there is always room for improvement." We are in a more solid position when we focus on improving our game over winning and accepting whatever happens along the way. This holds true for competitive golfers as well. The way to win is to improve. *Take care of the process and the results will take care of themselves.* Winning is a natural by-product of skill and focus applied in impeccable fashion (in combination with a good measure of factors we cannot control such as luck and the performance of others). If our focus shifts to winning or trying not to lose—when we get ahead in a match or start going low—we've moved away from the basis of our success. This paradox is a difficult one to grasp. Attachment to winning by not losing leads to risk aversion and heightened emotional reactivity. To win, all of our attention must be given to the task at hand. And this is all and always the shot sitting before us. This shot does not determine whether we win or lose—unless it is a critical final shot. Don't grasp directly for the victory. Feel, instead, the action of the moment. This shot. Now.

Research in sport psychology shows a task-orientation to be associated with more enjoyment, satisfaction, and intrinsic motivation. It's fine to be motivated to win as long as there is a strong task-orientation present. Ego-orientation can be beneficial if it leads to encouraging self-talk and images of success, provided these images don't become a preoccupation that interferes with present moment performance.

The downside of the ego-orientation is trying to avoid the social costs of losing. During my first stroke play club championship, I played rather poorly even by my own beginner standards. When the scores were posted at the end of the day, I held the highest score. My ego cringed. I worked with myself to put the round in context. This was, after all, my first competitive tournament and variation is the rule for the novice golfer. The next day, I tried to play as if yesterday hadn't happened. My approach shot to the 6th green from 120 yards landed 3 inches from the cup, offering me my first birdie on that hole. I was playing my best round ever! As fortune would have it, a thunderstorm was rolling in and the horn blew just as my group approached the green. Rather than playing out, my partners decided to pack it in. Thinking the storm would pass, I marked my ball and left with the group. The storm did not relent and the tournament was called for the day. What about my 3-inch birdie putt? I was informed my group would have to restart the round at the sixth several days later at the make-up date—local rules applied. I was horrified. I felt ripped off. "How dare they deny me my birdie!" My mind went on and on like this. I was emotional during practice before the round, feeling a mixture of anger and sadness—all ego. I considered leaving and not completing the round. I put these petty feelings aside and went to the sixth tee box. Instead of focusing on what I had lost (ego-orientation), I refocused on the game that gave me the birdie opportunity in the first place. I made par on that hole and went on to shoot my lowest round ever, besting my first-round score by 18 strokes and winning an honorable mention for most improved player!

Self-acceptance is the cure for excessive ego—the "disease of me." Too much ego-orientation speaks to a contingent self—as if our self-worth depends on the outcome of our golf game. As already mentioned, ego-orientation requires protection. Our self-esteem is on the line and at risk every time we stand over the ball. This can lead to extra anxiety in pressure situations. When the contingent self is active, fear won't be far away. When this happens, it's always possible to recommit ourselves to the process at hand and re-orient to the present: pre-shot routines, astute observation of our internal and external environments, quieting the talking mind as we swing. One study of elite athletes found they had strong self-acceptance. In this way, they were not basing their self-worth solely on their performance.

"Researchers have also pinpointed the fact that athletes with a high ego orientation and low self-confidence tend to experience the highest levels of anxiety before competition, leading to disrupted concentration and negative thinking. Generally, the opposite is true for those athletes with a task-orientation." Task-orientation embodies what is known as the *beginner's mind.* It is said that the beginner's mind knows many possibilities, the expert mind few. While we wish to develop expertise, we also want to remain open and curious about this moment. The beginner's mind doesn't think it knows it all, has seen it all—been there; done that. Instead the beginner's mind is oriented to the present: "What is happening right now?" The beginner's mind sees more, hears more, and feels more in any given moment because it is not prematurely committing to mental categories. Task-oriented athletes use the feedback available in any given moment to improve performance in the very near future.

We need confidence to sustain our efforts, although self-loathing can go a long way too but doesn't feel as good and doesn't get good results. Whether it is across a season, a round, or even within a hole, confidence is the glue that keeps attention together. When we are confident and focused on task-mastery rather than ego protection it is far easier to stay engaged and to avoid the kind of discouragement that impairs performance. Questions to ask yourself are: "What is my purpose?" That is, "Why do I play this game?" "How will I know if I am successful?" These questions can help to clarify purpose. If you find the answers to these questions tinged with ego concerns—such as looking good in front of others, glory over mastery, et cetera—you might want to revisit your sense of purpose. High presence of ego suggests that golfing and self-esteem have become dangerously confused. It is hard to be ego-driven without being egotistical—and thereby subject to destructive emotions when things don't go as planned. Ego-orientation requires protection and this protection requires energy—energy that could otherwise be available for performance. Our job is to disentangle *self* from action, and to give our undivided focus to the task at hand. You should play golf because you love to play golf. If you are using golf as means to bolster self-esteem, your problems exceed the help I can offer in this book—you'll probably need to check yourself into an insane asylum!

An inability to praise the accomplishments of others points to harmful ego-involvement. In golf, our opponent is not really our opponent. We are playing against par. In match play, we are seeking to play our best on each shot and each hole. Losing graciously never hurt anyone. It's good etiquette. It's also good mind etiquette. If we are inclined to judge others and put them down, we are likely to do the same to ourselves.

Of course, we all have our moments of ego and this is natural. Left unchecked, however, ego involvement can become a problem. Whenever you notice that this egotistical self has become activated, acknowledge it and move back into the process-orientation of the present moment action. "What do I need to do right now?" "What does this shot require?" Endeavor to give that shot your full attention, free from ego. If things go well and you win, hats off to you! There is nothing wrong with winning, vanquishing opponents, and looking good, so long as you don't *need* these things to happen in order to feel good about yourself. Our actions should be pure with no residue of self.

21. Freedom is Nothing More Than Telling Shame and Death to Go %#*! Themselves

The title of this chapter suggests that fear and shame are responsible for much, if pretty much all, of our misery. We are either afraid of some mortal danger, usually the very fact that we have to die someday, or we are afraid of looking bad in some way. Indeed, what could we be anxious about if we were not concerned with shame that comes up trying to protect our egos? What could rattle us if we were not afraid of death? Anxiety is part of our threat response system. It alerts us to potential danger. If we are anxious playing golf, we must ask ourselves: "What am I trying to protect?" Unless you've secured a bet with your house deed, there is likely nothing of mortal significance that will arise during a round of golf. To enjoy the aforementioned freedom, we must become more of a task-oriented rather than an ego-oriented golfer. This transition helps us to re-orient ourselves in a more fruitful direction that takes our self-worth off the table. Trying to protect the self from every conceivable threat makes us very vulnerable. We are out of control because we can be affected by what other people say and do and, on the golf course, by how we perform.

At a practical level, we can work with anxiety in the following way: Whenever anxiety arises and becomes part of your conscious awareness, seek clarification on what the anxiety is about. That is, what are the thoughts and images that are contributing to this feeling state? Be aware that anxiety may not always be obvious nerves, it can take subtle forms, such as tightening your grip or getting lost in conversations in your mind. If you can clarify the cause or causes, see if you can figure out what do about it. Ask yourself: "Why do I care?" If reasons can be identified, you can then ask, "Can I give up my attachment to these reasons?"

Consider this example. You've hit a green in regulation. You are nervous standing over your second putt, six feet away. In addition to being anxious, you are angry with yourself for leaving it this short. You miss the putt. Now you are even more frustrated with yourself as you proceed to three-putt and "blow" this opportunity to make par. To change this scenario, first you need to have sufficient awareness to notice the strong emotions that are suddenly with you on the green. Second, you can seek clarification. The missed second putt apparently violated some embedded rule of what "should have" happened. The violation of this rule apparently has implications for your score on the hole, your score on the round—of course—but it also seems to have something to do with your stature as a golfer. It might even have implications for your worth as a human being. These are the thoughts that may be circulating through your mind and such thoughts "feed" anxiety. Since the brain feels threatened by these rule violations, it will "authorize" anxiety. This anxiety tends to be self-perpetuating, feeding off itself. Left unchecked, this shame-based anxiety tends to interfere with performance. However, properly managed, the raw energy of anxiety can be recruited to improve performance.

Before Camilo Villegas hit his 6th hole approach shot into the water during the final round at the 2008 Tour Championship he was charging for the lead. He hit a good approach from the drop area and had a short putt to escape with a bogey. He missed this putt, winding up with a double bogey. The next hole was more trouble: a bogey on 7. Villegas was obviously shaken by this meltdown. His caddy said to him, 'You ain't going to give up on me. We can still do it,'" Villegas said of his caddy: "He was probably the only one believing that at that point." Villegas did not allow embarrassment or shame to interfere with his performance. Instead, he refocused his attention ever more fiercely and birdied the next two holes, and three of the next four. He went on to win the Tour Champion at East Lake capturing second in the FedEx Cup and taking home $4.26 million. To pull off this feat, Villegas had to play one shot at a time, assigning each shot the same level of care, no one shot more valuable than any other, and in the process of not trying he was able to pull off this come from behind victory.

Clark Perry said, "Most golfers have bought into the golf-course architect's evil plot to sabotage their confidence and self-esteem." Most of us don't wait until the end of 18 holes to measure our level of success. We examine it after each hole and determine how well we are playing according to par. This constant examination of success is the trap that the architect has laid in conjunction with this evil twin, the television commentator. At every tournament, year after year, we are reminded that "this is a big putt, because it is to save par; miss it and the player will drop a shot," which implies that one shot is more important than another.

Every golf instructor will tell you and has probably already told you that each shot is equally important or, better yet, equally unimportant. Dr. Bob Rotella urges his students to assign a low-level of importance to any given shot. And by extension we should assign a low level of importance to any hole, any round, any tournament, or any *thing*. By assigning anything other than a low level of importance to the outcome of the shot we are diverting our valuable limited attention resource away from what it needs to do most—make the present shot! If we become anxious, the brain will allocate resources to something that it can't do anything about—what happened on the last hole or its worry about what might happen on the next hole (I can't do anything about that now). Beyond helping us to be alert and concentrated on the shot, any other attention devoted to outcome becomes worry. The more we focus on the score, the more chance that we will score poorly. Perry reminds us that if we can treat "each shot as an isolated game with no history" we can come to regard this moment as a challenge to make our best shot.

22. Why Didn't I Kneel More Deeply to Accept You?

It might be obvious to say that negative feelings feel bad. The awfulness of negative feelings makes sense when we think about their purpose: They evolved to give us an evolutionary advantage. Take discouragement, for example, it provides feedback that a goal cannot be reached and we would be better off investing our time and energy resources elsewhere. Our ancestors who were good at allocating their limited resources probably had adaptive advantages in the environment of 100,000 years ago. Today, however, we have an aversion, even a phobia, to anything in the negative spectrum. I believe this is largely conditioned by culture. Just watch television commercials. There is a remedy for every condition known to humankind, from headaches to heart disease, from eczema to erectile dysfunction, from diabetes to depression. We can't help but feel deficient if we have any of these or, by extension, feel bad at any time.

Negative feelings will inevitably arise in the course of our golf game: disappointment, anger, frustration, and even sadness. Can we embrace these feelings instead of continuing to indulge them or trying to get rid of them? Can we, like our successful ancestors, use them to adaptive advantage? Can we remember their original purpose: To give us important information that we can use to make adjustments to our life in this moment. And when this moment is playing golf, the arising of a negative feeling is an occasion to pause and reflect: "What can I learn from this moment?" We can start to cultivate the habit of trading self-criticism—often the cause of negative feelings—for curiosity and even gratitude.

Some of the negative feelings that arise while playing are unlikely to have any utility because they are products of faulty beliefs such as believing we should be much more expert than we actually are. They don't contain any actionable information so our best option is to accept them without acting on them. Accepting like this opens a space in our game where the negative feelings can be without interfering with performance. We can even come to value the difficulty, as the poet Rilke did when he said, "why didn't I kneel more deeply to accept you, you nights of anguish?" By accepting, it is possible to be happy while experiencing adverse feelings. To pull off this feat, requires us to "undo" our cultural conditioning. Americans tend to confuse happiness with comfort, ease, and freedom from adversity, but happiness does not have to depend on these. When negative feelings are investigated in the here and now, we can see they really have nothing to do with our happiness, unless we go out of our way to build a bridge between them. Without this bridge, a poor shot is just that, a poor shot. The FIT mind can accept this and leverage all of its attention to the next shot and maximize the chances of a better result. If the result is not better, the FIT mind can try again, and then again. At no point does it base its happiness on the outcome of the shot. It doesn't get caught in the trap of tying its wellbeing to the trajectory of a golf shot.

23. Stress is an Orange: Juice It!

> I had big nerves today. But you have to have nerves. If you aren't nervous then you don't try hard enough.—Carlos Franco

It's a set up to think that we will never be nervous while playing golf or that the great players never get nervous. They do. The difference between the great players and the rest of us is that they know how to handle these feelings. Feelings are vital juice when managed properly. Nervousness stems from desire; we want something and are afraid that we may not get it. Anxiety comes from perceived threats to our wellbeing and the need to protect the self. What if you imagined that desire as an orange? Then you could juice it.

Lawrence Olivier was considered the greatest actor of his generation. He would throw up each night before a performance. Certainly, he knew his skills and the accolades bestowed upon him, yet he was still nervous. Fortunately, you don't need ice water in your veins to perform well in pressure situations. It is natural to be nervous when facing a putt for birdie. The interpretation of this nervous energy is crucial. If we start talking to ourselves about the nervousness, allowing the mind to generate stories about poor past performance and worry about outcome, we could be in trouble. This type of "talk" can impair performance. If we resist the temptation to interpret the nervousness and instead focus on the bodily sensations that accompany it, we can begin to "juice" it and harvest the benefits from this energy.

A classic psychology experiment demonstrates the power of interpretation. Subjects were unknowingly injected with adrenaline—the very stuff of arousal. They were then placed in different situations that provided different contexts for this physiological experience. Subjects would interpret what they felt as anger in angry situations and as joy in joyful ones. Interpretation is key.

Out of control anxiety in competition can lead to a narrowing of attention and a lack of cognitive flexibility. We can become illogical and rash, making poor decisions. If you are anxious about protecting your score, then your play will change to reflect this. Focusing on avoiding mistakes keeps the concept of "mistake" paramount; the experience of anxiety might introduce muscle tension and constricted attention that may lead to poorer performance—for example, fat shots due to deceleration. In fact, anxiety may often lead to deceleration because the anxiety is trying to "protect" us, and this protection comes in the form of muscle tension that slows the rhythm of our swing. Anxiety can lead to giving our body conflicting instructions; the nervousness says, "Hey, wait a minute ... are you sure it's that much effort?" That question leads to deceleration and a poor shot execution. This defensive, anxiety-laced approach to playing can undermine confidence and actually lead to the feared outcome.

Anxiety is both a trait and a state. Anyone can get into an anxious state and there are some of us who are more prone to trait anxiety due to genetic factors and early learning. For those of us with a predisposition towards anxiety, like Laurence Olivier, there is an added challenge since anxiety will be common and not just a passing state. Trait anxiety is often connected with perfectionism and this can lead to being highly self-critical, focusing on the negative aspects of any situation. Being anxiety-prone means being more attentive to threatening elements in the environment. On the course, this may translate to focusing on out of bounds markers, hazards, and other "dangers" in the environment. Due to a combination of anxiety-impaired performance and the imagery of visualizing the hazard, we are more likely to put the shot where we fear it might go. What a lovely confirmation! Anxious performance then creates biased memory. Recalling that anxiety is part of our threat response system, we will have a better memory for negative outcomes than positive outcomes.

Even neutral situations may be perceived as threatening when we are highly anxious. Anxiety influences the filters through which we see and experience the world. Again, this process depends entirely on *interpretation*. These interpretations are often biased or simply wrong. Interpretations are never facts. You can always revise interpretations, an especially good idea when anxiety pushes them towards inaccuracy. An accurate and rational perception says: "I hit the shot into the hazard" may be followed by an inaccurate and irrational interpretation: "Therefore my round is ruined; I'm a terrible golfer; why did I ever take this game up?; I'm an idiot; I'm going to quit!" We spend our mental lives indoctrinating ourselves with these interpretations and we could just as readily indoctrinate ourselves with more supportive interpretations: "Well, that shot sucked, but it's just one shot; I can do better than that; now I'll focus on what I have to do next." End of story. We are better off when we can prevent our interpretations from spiraling out of control into irrational, negative thinking.

Worry is closely related to anxiety and is our mind's attempt to control the future through obsessive focus. This strategy may appear to work because the process of worrying *seems* to make us feel better, at least temporarily. Worry can become reinforcing in this way. Remember though, we can't think our way out of a problem that thinking got us into in the first place. Worry is not actually helping us to control outcomes. Focusing on the future can be beneficial to the extent that it helps us to prepare for that future. However, with worry and its extreme form—rumination—we quickly go beyond the point of diminishing returns and are engaged in worry for worry's sake—worry that takes on a life of its own.

A better strategy is to turn worry from an adversary into an ally. We can ask the question: "What's the threat here?" It may be something that we want to have—victory, looking good, making a score—or something that we don't want to have—embarrassment, poor performance. If we didn't *care*, there would be no threatening *feelings*. So, nervousness points to caring or, in other words, desire. We want something. What is this? What is being threatened here? Is there anything other than ego concerns on the line? Likely not. If there is no actual threat, then we can work with the energy of the situation and tell the worry to stand down.

There is a well-established law in physiological psychology that portrays the relationship between arousal and performance. This law can be envisioned as an inverse U-shaped curve. At low levels of arousal, performance is low. There's just not enough juice to move us toward any goals. You don't score well because you never got out of bed in the morning. At high levels of arousal, performance is also low. Too much arousal and we become impaired by emotion and cannot perform at our best. In between these two extremes is the middle range: Moderate arousal leading to peak performance.

Avoiding mind *talk* will help to keep the juice of nervous energy in the moderate range. By turning attention to the sensations in the body—the actual energy of the nervousness—we can accept what is happening in the present moment. If we wish we weren't nervous or see the nervousness as an obstacle, we are resisting the experience.

Resistance leads to increased tension and may actually push arousal higher into the impairment range.

The more familiar and comfortable we can become with the bodily "signatures" of arousal, the more we can use it to our advantage and prevent it from spiraling out of control into high levels of arousal. We can learn to welcome this energy and to integrate it into present moment awareness to maximize our golf performance. This requires staying away from the *talk* aspects of mind and staying focused on the *feel* and *touch* aspects. When we do the Body Scan exercise on a regular basis, we are training the mind to become familiar and comfortable with the juice of peak performance (see Appendix). Frequent practice can help us to extend the performance curve where we can still perform well even with higher levels of arousal. This can be especially helpful in competitive situations where arousal is likely to be high.

Sally was an excellent amateur player, having placed second in a statewide amateur tournament the year before. She came to me to because of excessive nervousness when playing in tournaments. She saw the nervousness as a problem that she needed to get rid of. We discussed the relationship between expectations—with perceived consequences—and the arising of anxiety. She learned the basics of Mind Fitness to retrieve her mind from the place of future expectations to help limit the impact of anxiety in the present. She was encouraged to see nervousness as inevitable and no big deal. She was shown the inverse U-shaped curve. Understanding this curve helped her to put anxiety in context, one in which it was embraced rather than resisted. She saw how all her self-talk activity propelled her arousal into the danger zone, reducing her performance. She learned to befriend the experience in her body, to take this juice and use it to empower her performance.

The classic model is usually shown as an inverted "U" shaped curve. However, this model is not exactly accurate because performance will drop off precipitously at a certain point of arousal and not gradually as the inverted U suggests.

What will help you to stay in the optimal performance zone? For some of us, it may be lessening the focus on competition; for others, it may be enhancing it. When we can uncouple our sense of well-being from performance outcome, we create a space in which to juice the energy of competition. We can play as if our lives depended upon it without staking our lives upon it.

Properly *juicing* the orange can improve performance as suggested by Claude Harmon talking with George Plimpton in *The Bogey Man* about the *adrenaline quota.* This "juice" can lead to an extra 30 yards on a swing. He relays a story of Lee Trevino in the 1967 U.S. Open: "Trevino's all hopped up, crazy strong, and he knows it, so he grabs himself an eight iron—instead of the five his caddy suggested—and hits the flag with it. Well, imagine where a five iron would have taken him."

One theory suggests we each have our individual zones of optimal functioning. For some, optimal performance will come with an edge and for others it is the absence of an edge. For some mild anger and irritation will help, while for others these feelings will get in the way. In other words, one size does not fit all. You must know yourself and discover what works best for you.

Throughout, interpretation is key. If the stuff of anxiety, stress, and arousal can be interpreted as performance juice, we are likely to perform better, stay in our optimal performance zone, and enjoy our game more. The FIT mind is more adept at recognizing unhelpful interpretations and revising them or simply turning attention away from them. When worrisome thoughts about the future arise, we can return attention to the present without getting into an elaborate analysis of whether the thoughts are justified. In addition to returning attention to the action of moment, we can work directly with the juice. Monitoring breathing is another key. When the juice is strong, breathing will be affected. Taking a full and diaphragm-engaged breath (see Appendix for instructions) can be helpful to release residual tension. Focusing on the bodily signatures of the juice goes hand-in-hand with releasing tension. You can imagine your breath breathing into and out of the area where you most feel the strain. This is a proactive way to engage work with the juice. Another helpful strategy is to retrain your focus on something happening in the concrete present. The bodily signatures of arousal are part of this concrete present, and so too are the sights and sounds of being on the course. Commit to your pre-shot routine. Breathing, focusing attention, and reducing threat can keep the juice in the optimal performance zone.

24. Different Day Different Body

> The mystery of golf is that nobody can master it. You can shoot a good score today, but can you do it tomorrow.—Curtis Strange

As a collection of dynamic energies, the body changes ceaselessly. Even at the microscopic level, we are always changing. Our atoms change over year-by-year and almost all of our cells every seven years or so. While we may have the appearance of stability, change is the order of the day. At the macroscopic level, change is also the order of the day.

One day we play fluid and relaxed, the next constrained and tense.

What does it mean to play relaxed? The term relaxation conjures up many different images, some of which may not be helpful while playing golf. What we really mean by relaxed is getting out of our own way so we can do what we know how to do. We relinquish the excess effort that can bias the swing. We "relax" into the swing and thereby into the moment. This is when we get our best results.

A variation of the different day, different body observation is the different time of day, different body. I played a tournament match in the middle of the afternoon starting at 3:30. I was somewhat exhausted from a long week of work. I struggled on the front 9, shooting terribly. Fortunately, I was only 3 down at the turn. Making the turn at 5:30 I noticed my energy rising and my play coming together. I shot brilliantly—for me—on the back and won my match 2 and 1. The body has a biological clock known as the circadian rhythm that goes through two cycles each day. The low point occurs in the middle of the night and again in the middle of the afternoon. At the low point, we may experience sleepiness as body temperature drops. The effects of this rhythm will be more pronounced when the body is already tired. The circadian rhythm can therefore tell us if we are well rested, nourished, and hydrated.

The situation for female golfers highlights the different day different body principle. This is the "Period Factor." Jill McGill tells Rick Reilly: "Your timing just isn't there. Your body feels kind of out of balance." Another pro, Wendy Ward suggests, "it's a rhythm thing. It just throws you all off. I mean, I've tried to psych myself out of it. I've tried to pretend I don't have it. I'm like, 'this does not exist. I'm the same person. Same clubs. Same swing. Nothing is new.' But then you get out there and you can't." While men don't have a period to contend with, we all have bodily variations that can affect play.

"Feel" is an elusive prize in golf. In a Golf Digest article, Arnold Palmer writing at 79 discusses the "Feel of a Good Shot." He notes that feel is the most perplexing part of golf. His feel for putting has just returned after a 25-year absence. Players try to court *feel* in a variety of creative and sometimes bizarre ways. Gene Sarazen plunged his hands into hot water; Hogan recommended drinking ginger ale. Putters get weighted with tape. Arnie concludes that these gimmicks don't really work. He also notes "instructors don't seem to understand it very well. In fact, great touch is often written off simply as 'talent.'" Arnie notes that the mechanics of feel depend upon subtle variations in club head speed—perhaps a couple of miles per hour—and adjusting the swing path by a degree or two.

Feel seems to also arise from the confidence we bring to our game. Feel, I would venture, is there at all times, just as the sun is always present behind a wall of clouds on a stormy day. Our job is to clear the clouds away so that feel can emerge. In this way, feel is not adding something new, but working to remove obstacles. And this work must not be "effort" in the typical sense that we understand effort. The work is releasing into the present moment. It's more of an "allowing" than any particular "doing." Having made this distinction there are ways we can increase the likelihood that we'll get access to good feel. Being relaxed and in a good mood can facilitate, although by no means guarantee, access. Heightened awareness can also facilitate access to feel. Being aware that we are tense and hurried—two obstacles to feel—can help us to relax and slow down. I like to do some juggling before teeing off. This simple activity coordinates hand-eye movement and helps me concentrate. It also takes me out of any obsessive golf-related thoughts or nervousness about the round. If you can't juggle or are not interested in learning, find some other activity that can serve the same purpose.

I played one of the best front nines of my life one evening after attending a very humorous talk. The laughter relaxed my body and helped me to play naturally. I shot well below my handicap.

Feel, as Arnie Palmer bemoans, will come and go. There is no remedy for that and beware any promises to the contrary. Variation is something we have to accept. Yet again, this acceptance does not have to be resignation. There are things we can do when feel is elusive, including sticking to routines, recruiting imagination, and avoiding interfering self-talk. I also caution against becoming superstitious about the associations that accompany a good feel day. I rather doubt it was your lucky hat or shirt that did it. I am dubious that any gimmick will reliably produce results. Establishing Mind Fitness is perhaps the most reliable way to produce access to *feel* because we are establishing actual skills. The more aware we are of our minds and the more connected we are to our bodies, the better we will be able to access the magic of feel.

25. The Whole is Greater than the Sum of the Parts

We can view the world from different vantage points, each focusing on a different aspect of reality. One of these ways of looking at the world focuses on the form and structure of things. For golf, this includes equipment, clothes, grip, and stance. These are the materials forms that we bring to bear on our game. Once we start moving, we can rotate attention to the view of mechanics with a focus on the dynamics of the swing path, acceleration, deceleration, follow-through, and so forth. We can also take an organic view of our game, seeing it as a developmental process with a natural progression. Finally, we can seek to put our game in the big picture of our history of golfing and even our lives. This big picture view helps us to avoid reducing golf to its parts—the positions of elbows during swings, the pencil marks on score cards, and the putts that either go in or do not.

We can view "golf" as a whole, as an entity unto itself. Contained within this whole are all our golf-related experiences. We can also break golf down into smaller wholes. Each round of golf is a whole, each hole within a round is a whole; each shot within a hole is a whole. As a whole, or *holon*, we can come to see this shot as something deserving of and commanding our full attention in the present. If we compromise the holon by breaking it up into pieces, we'll miss the bigger picture. Breaking things down cuts us off from important information and can lead to the following types of rationalizations: "If I miss this shot I've bogeyed and thereby botched the hole." This violates the holon of the shot. A round of golf is a collection of holons, preferably as few as possible.

See what happens if you view your game from the whole of each shot. From this perspective, each shot assumes a relative low level of importance. After all, it's just one shot. What does this whole require? Can it receive your *whole* attention in this moment? By viewing each shot as a holon, one poor shot does not contaminate the next shot since that would violate the integrity of its wholeness. In fact, the last shot does not exist any longer since it only lives in memory, and absolutely has no relevance for the next shot—short of any actionable information gleaned from that shot, such as the feel of the rough, the speed of the greens, the play of the wind, and so forth. See what happens if you view your game from the whole of each hole—both the poorly-played holes and even the well-played holes. If we allow excitement over a well-played hole to set up expectations for future performance, they'll likely be disappointed. The expectations themselves may actually get in the way of performing. Just as with each shot and each hole, there is a holon for the round, for the season, and for a lifetime playing golf.

26. Don't Take Yourself So Seriously

> What's the record for the number of golf balls lost in nine holes? And why doesn't someone invent a tee that you can slit your wrists with.—Carl Hiaasen

Golf makes me want to cry sometimes. Expectations set this up. Unexpected results are the catalyst. If you're so frustrated you're about to cry, you're taking this all too seriously and even if you are a serious golfer, you don't need to take yourself so seriously. If you're so frustrated you become angry, you're taking this all too seriously. If you can get to the point when you laugh at a topped ball, a hook into the woods and a slice into a condo, then you are moving towards liberation.

Look at the assumptions that frame your expectations. What are your "rules of engagement?" What are the perceived consequences for not doing what you wanted or expected to do on a particular golf shot? Each rule gets in the way of joy. If we don't take ourselves too seriously, then we can enjoy our game, even if we don't play well. George Byran IV shot a 63 in the final round of the Southern Amateur. Before doing so, he told himself "go out there and have fun." Joy may even arise if we allow it. After all, golf is a special experience. It is a game that takes us over the face of the earth, seeing shades of green and configurations of grass that sometimes defy belief.

At the very least we can breathe the outdoor air and behold the sky. We can walk and feel the earth beneath our feet. The very *opportunity* to be golfing at all may be a sufficient occasion for joy. Such joy is available in any moment, regardless of how well we are playing in that moment. All moments hold the potential for delight if we can let go of our insistence that things be a particular way. Joy is especially available if we can uncouple our value as a human being from how the game goes. Simply put: less ego equals more joy.

27. Violent Emotion is a Kind of Insanity

Becoming infuriated after a poor shot and engaging in self-damnation is a form of psychosis—it's a departure from reality. Like the Vulcans of Star Trek, I view violent emotions as a psychotic-like process because they go well beyond the adaptive function of feelings. They are divorced from reality, as the mind is engaged in a terrible story about what just happened and its awful imagined implications for the future. Often, it seems we just condemn ourselves with no particular agenda for the future other than "celebrating" our odious worthlessness. The comedian Lewis Black said that "golf was a game designed for people who don't hate themselves enough in their daily lives." The shot has occurred; beating ourselves up over it is not going to change that outcome.

Self-condemnation is also divorced from reality because we leverage expectations for expertise that we simply don't have. We get suckered by the occasional excellent shot and mistakenly use these shots as the reference standard for our game.

Sport psychology recognizes the destructiveness of anger: "An angry, out-of-control athlete or coach cannot perform at the best during competition." The research literature shows no benefit for anger. At what point does anger become "out-of-control"? Can anger ever be helpful? Our cultural images of anger probably don't help the situation. In the 1970s, primal scream therapy was popular and we've often gotten the message that venting anger is better than bottling it up inside. While suppressing emotions is not healthy, venting them through impulsive angry behavior is not a solution. When we get angry and release it through yelling, punching a pillow, or driving our seven-iron into the ground, we feel a temporary state of relief. This relief is reinforcing. Even though the outburst feels good it is likely not helpful for your game. "Research shows that aggressive behavior does not reduce the likelihood of subsequent aggressive behavior; in fact, it sometimes increases it frequency and intensity. Expressing anger physically, even in a controlled way, is not a good self-management strategy to use or to teach athletes."

Anger directed at our equipment or ourselves is equally disruptive. The energy that goes into beating ourselves up or club pounding is energy that is no longer available for your game. Some athletes, like Tiger, can use brief bursts of anger as a course correction. The anger apparently remains at the feeling level for him and does not become a disruptive emotion. Legendary NFL coach Bill Parcels put it this way, "If you lose your cool, no matter what the provocation, you're giving the other side of the table a diagram on how to push your buttons." Even when there is no opponent in golf, the game itself can stand as the most formidable opponent. The game already knows how to push our buttons. Getting angry only gives in to this. What is to be gained by this, outside of the temporary but costly relief from the outburst? Anger is an "expensive" way to handle frustrating situations. It costs emotional energy that could otherwise be devoted to focus and enjoyment of the game. Outbursts only justify the self-condemnations that triggered the anger in the first place. This type of anger is dangerous because it feeds off itself. When we are angry we are allowing ourselves to be pushed around by the beliefs that underlie the emotion. We sometimes rationalize the outburst because part of the perception is true, "I *did* triple-bogey that hole." Even if the beliefs are true in some sense, they are irrelevant when we are committed to a present-moment focused game. Furthermore, we wouldn't treat another person or an animal in the way we just treated ourselves.

Instead of being angry, be assertive. Assertive golfers are "intense, confident, never give up, and constantly challenge themselves to reach optimal performance." In fact, the prevailing mood of elite athletes usually runs cool rather than the hot of anger.

The Mind FIT golfer knows how to temper emotions in ways that are less expensive. When the feeling of anger arises in the body, we can move our focus to these bodily sensations and pay curious attention to them in short circuit a full-blown emotional reaction.

George Plimpton describes the unfortunate outburst of his pro playing partner, Tom Bruno, after missing a putt: "But on the way to the next tee, stringing along, he suddenly swerved off the path into the woods. He disappeared. We could hear him moving through the underbrush. I thought perhaps he had gone in there to take a pee. Then we heard an odd bopping sound. Someone looked and said, "My god, he's in there beating his driver against a stump!" His club mangled and unusable, Bruno puts the club back in his bag anyway, as Plimpton describes as a reminder of the "melancholy crisis" in the woods. Plimpton laments the fate of the golfer. "Lack of emotional control costs the professional in his golf score as well. Golf cannot be played in anger, or in any mood of emotional excess. Half the golf balls struck by amateurs are hit if not in rage surely in bewilderment, or gloom, or in cynicism, or even hysterically—all of those emotional excesses which must be contained by the professional."

Plimpton goes on to review the sordid history of professional golfers who gave vent to anger. There are tales of golfers who knocked themselves out by punching themselves in the head with clubs, rocks, and fists. Some of these incidents clearly have a psychotic, out-of-touch-with-reality feeling to them. The golfer who would beat his hand against a tree shouting, "Take that ... that'll teach you." Or the golfer who attempted to drown his offending club in the water hazard. Or the golfer who would attach his putter to a string and drag it from the car as he drove along the highway in an attempt to "punish it." Or the golfer who would jump into the crowd to berate spectators who had been critical of him. Bobby Jones, of course, had a temper that he learned to control at age 19. For him, this "spirit" was a great energy to be respected and harnessed.

28. Go With The Flow!

Flow is the term that psychologist Mihaly Csikszentmihalyi (pronounced *chick-sent-me-hi*) coined to describe the state of being completely absorbed in an activity. This absorption lacks self-consciousness and is pleasurable. The perception of time is altered. Flow arises in situations where there is an optimal balance between challenge and skills. Too much challenge with insufficient skills results in feeling overwhelmed, anxious, or worried; too little challenge with sufficient skills results in boredom, even apathy. Flow lies in between. Flow is described as a rare and fleeting experience that depends on the right match between the external and internal environments.

Unfortunately, turning off self-consciousness is a supreme challenge and a situation that, as the rarity of flow testifies, does not occur all that frequently. Sometimes this state has been likened to being on automatic pilot. However, I think it is helpful to distinguish automatic pilot from an absence of self-consciousness. Automatic pilot suggests a trance state. You can drive down the highway with no self-consciousness, but the mind is not absorbed into the activity of the moment. It may be having imaginary conversations, rehearsing the future, etc. The flow-oriented lack of self-consciousness implies full contact and absorption into the activity of the moment.

Mind Fitness can make flow more available. As mentioned above, flow arises when challenges are balanced with skills. To pursue mind FIT flow we can use attention to make any situation a situation with sufficient interest to support flow. Flow happens in the present, as the past and future drop away. Flow tends to arise when we focus on a small and specific target, such as this little white ball going to that precise spot on the green. Mind FIT flow is not caught up in things that it cannot control. It is process-oriented. The FIT mind *can* control attention; it is prepared for the action at hand. The FIT mind does not judge its game or itself in the middle of the game. Once the round is complete there will be time for reflection and non-ego-based appraisal of performance with the opportunity to integrate what has been learned. Meanwhile, mind FIT flow has better access to the rhythm of the game. The FIT mind can enjoy the swing, the walking, and the overall experience of playing golf. Mind FIT flow is *feel*-based. Mind FIT flow is not about swing thoughts but, rather, the embodied swing. If we are in flow, we increase the likelihood of having fun. Indeed, golf is a game and, as such, it holds the opportunity to be fun.

GOLF TECHNIQUE

This section focuses specifically on golf techniques, including learning how to *swing like you don't care*. Each of the entries in this section will take the principles enumerated in the first three sections and apply them on the golf course. Practicing these techniques can help to improve your game.

29. Kill Hope

> Golf books and golf magazines sell like crazy because every player is searching for the formula, the secret, the code, the grail—how do I conquer this impossible, godforsaken game? … And the more you read, the more hopelessly muddled you become.—Carl Hiaasen

We golfers are desperate for something—anything—that might get our game to be more consistent or take it to the next level. We are vulnerable to hope and golf books and magazines exploit this vulnerability.

Here are some typical *Golf Magazine* taglines:

"My plan for winning scores: The foolproof way to pick the right shot"

"Crush it!: 13 Ways to Plan and Pure Every Shot"

"Play pitch shots with perfect distance"

"Fix your game: Start to play consistently better rounds today"

"4 Foolproof Steps to Hit Greens"

"Hit more greens and get it close"

"Gain 17 yards now!"

"Turn your swing into a Tour Swing"

"Unlock your 300 Yard Drive"

"3 Simple keys to extra distance, greater consistency, pinpoint accuracy"

"QUICK FIXES: 15 More Yards in 5 Minutes"

Since I read these articles it sounds like I should be on the PGA Tour by now! Hiaasen provides more sage advice: "Most players drift from weekend to weekend in a fog of anxious flux; they play well in streaks and then, for no plain reason, fall apart. They are seldom more than one poor round away from stammering desperations, and to these unhinged souls every golf article dangles the most precious enticement: hope."

I often encourage my students and patients to "kill hope." This may seem like an odd suggestion but think about it. Hope often arises when we confront circumstances we have faced before, yet we "hope" the outcome will be different. A popular definition of insanity is to engage in the same activity over and over again yet expecting different results? It might also be difficult not to confuse hope with faith. We can have faith that hard work and practice will improve our games, but this is different from hoping—today will be different!— because faith has a basis in reality. Hope arises when we plunk down a couple of hundred dollars on some device that will adjust our aura so that we'll sink more ten footers. Of course, it's good to be optimistic that we will play well and this attitude may in fact contribute directly to playing well. However and again, this is different from hope. Hope shows up and expects something that is not grounded in reality. Do your game a favor and kill hope.

The first step for reckoning with hope is to normalize it—we are all susceptible. Next, rather than hoping we can set our sights on patience and a grounded understanding of the difficulty that faces us: Golf is an extraordinarily difficult game. It is going to take time to improve. There is no quick and easy fix. Progress is not linear; it ebbs and flows. It's fine to read golf magazines and we may even pick up a helpful tip, but we need to gird ourselves against unrealistic hope for the instantaneous transformation that we've been promised. It's not that the tips and instruction in golf magazines are not helpful—they can be. The problem is that we can find our heads filled with new swing thoughts, which will actually lower performance in the short-term. If our mind is engaged with these swing thoughts, it won't be on the swing. Ultimately, we need to swing without thinking. Crestfallen because our game has not been saved, we abandon the technique and feel dismal.

Here is a representative article. The cover features Vijay in the various stages of a swing with the headline: "Your New Swing Starts Here! Power and Control Vijay's Way." Mr. Singh says in the article: "If your swing is inconsistent, or you can't seem to put together two good shots in a row, try my new takeaway, then see if you can copy each of my positions on the pages that follow." I found myself enthralled with the promise of swinging like the 2008 Fedex Cup $10 million champion. But then I said, "Wait a minute, this is *his* swing, which is right for his body, not mine; it's right for his level of development as an elite, Hall of Fame golfer. I think a golf swing is as unique as a signature. If I write Vijay's name on my checks, it's fraud. Why would copying his swing be any different? He reports an increase of 10.5 yards off the tee, 5 percent more fairways, and 5.5 percent more greens in regulation by using this new takeaway. These are impressive numbers for improvement at his level, but would we see similar transformations in our own game? Likely not. In fact, if you copied these forms, your performance would likely go down until you were able to incorporate the change at an unconscious level and even then they may be inappropriate for you: This won't be your swing.

Tour player Paul Goydos (interviewed in the same Golf Magazine issue as the Vijay article) talks about being a better golf at 44 than he was a 24. He says, "I approached golf the wrong way. I said, 'Show me how to do this,' when I should have said, 'Teach me what you know.' Then, instead of copying someone, take that information and apply it. Make it yours." Goydos is distinguishing technique—what the golf magazines offer—from skill. From Goydos's perspective, golf magazines appeal to the 24-year-old in us rather than the mature 44-year-old. We must develop skills, not import techniques from hyperbolic golf tip feature articles.

30. Normal Curve

> Nothing goes down slower than a golf handicap.—Bobby Nichols.

It takes a lot of work to be an average golfer. Everyone, it seems, entertains fantasies of being a great golfer. On occasion we can all hit a great shot and there may be little to distinguish us from a PGA Tour Professional—on that one shot, that one hole. Folk wisdom cautions that even a blind squirrel can find a nut on occasion. The average golfer scores around 100 (98.3 according to the National Golf Foundation). If we assume that talent and the ability to score in golf follows a normal distribution, we should see the classic bell curve for scoring.

For the sake of this example, let's assume the standard deviation—a calculation for variability within a population—for the population of golfers is 10 shots. This would mean that 68 percent of all golfers—the fat, middle part of the bell curve—score between 110 and 90: the average range from low to high. The golf normal curve is actually a little skewed to the left because the high end of average is more like 119 strokes. If you can break 90, you are doing better than 75 percent of other golfers (because you are doing better than the really high average players too). If you can break 80, you are doing better than 95 percent of all golfers. If you can score 70 or better, you are in the top 1 percent of all golfers. Given that there are close to a million members of the USGA, there would be approximately 10,000 scratch golfers in the USGA. Of these, only 125 card-carrying members on the PGA Tour. However, there are 28.7 million golfers in the United States most whom. are not members of the USGA. These statistics leave us playing in relative mediocrity. These statistics can be a sobering antidote to professional golf fantasies and help us to put our game in a context, which will lead to more enjoyment and less frustration. The pros we see on television are not a suitable comparison group. We should admire them, not compare ourselves to them.

It takes a lot of work to move a handicap index and the handicap formula itself reflects an understanding of this by allowing for substantial variability in scores. In this way, one bad round does not affect the handicap index. Understanding how golf-scoring averages are distributed can help us evaluate our game in a saner context. These numbers can help to undermine hope and discourage grandiose fantasies that arise from hitting a good golf shot or having an exceptional round.

We can also think about the statistical concept of regression to the mean. This principle tells us that exceptional performance is just that, exceptional, and that future performance is likely to move towards average. Matt Cassel, Tom Brady's replacement in the 2008 season, set a New England Patriot's team record by having two consecutive 400-yard games (an accomplishment that Brady and Drew Bledsoe could not boast at the time). His next game was not 400-yards. He was regressing towards the mean. The takeaway message here is not to set yourself up with unreasonable expectations. Rather, build in a lot of room for variance in performance. Your handicap allows for this, and regression to the mean demands this. Regression to the mean also works in the opposite direction. If you have been playing terribly, you can expect an improvement in performance as your scores rise back towards your average. Enjoy playing well but don't expect it to continue uninterrupted; understand that poor play is temporary and will be followed by better play.

31. Frustration = Variation x Resistance

> The equipment can't save you from yourself. On a good day, a good golfer will shoot lights-out using any set of clubs. On a bad day, a bad golfer will butcher the easiest course in the country with $2000 worth of plasma-welded hardware in his bag.—Carl Hiaasen

Variation is a fact of golf. "Ever play 'Ray-Ray golf'? One hole you play like Ray Floyd, and the next you play like Ray Charles." Frustration is directly related to our ability to accept variability. Thus, we can derive the formula: Frustration = Variation multiplied by Resistance: F = V x R. Think of resistance as a lack of acceptance for any particular outcome. Things will change from day to day. One day you'll play great, the next day not so great with no apparent reason for the difference. The state of your body may have changed. Or the change may be due to simple variability based upon your level of skill. Even Tour pros see variability in how they play from day to day, tournament to tournament, season to season. If they didn't, scores would be clustered at the top instead of distributed; cuts would have to be a few strokes from the leader instead of about ten.

When we don't factor in variability, we are bound to be frustrated with what arises. We will be frustrated, angry, demoralized: "What the hell is wrong with me? I was playing so well yesterday!" Perfectionism makes no room for variability, and why it's destructive to our game.

As the above formula implies, the relationship between variation and frustration is not additive but multiplicative. Frustration is compounded by the interaction of change and resistance to change. The recommended corresponding formula for F = V x R is F = V/A, "A" is acceptance. The less we resist, the less frustrated we will be become and the more enjoyment we will have. This may appear like a paradox, but see if it is true. Once a shot is executed it cannot be undone. You can't take it back. Acceptance is the only sane option. Let's say on a given day there are seven units of variability—out of ten—and a moderate level of resistance, say a six. Therefore, frustration is seven times six or forty-two (F = 7 x 6). If instead, variability is divided by acceptance (E=7/6) or a frustration quotient of 1.17, which is preferable to a frustration quotient of 42 that stems from resistance.

We may also have difficulty accepting conditions—the wind for instance, or the rain that comes along with that wind, the speed of the greens or the divot in the green that steered your ball away from the hole. Can all conditions be accepted without resistance? It may be even harder for us to accept, or to even notice, the variations within ourselves. Whether we notice them or not, we'll still be bumping into them. If we cannot accept that our body is tired, stiff, or out of sync, we will be compounding our frustration by pushing against ourselves even harder.

Mind Fitness equips us to cope with the inevitable variations of golfing. We can ride the waves of variation without compounding resistance and open the way for enjoyment over frustration. When we are fully in the moment we are by default in acceptance and such acceptance allows things to be as they are.

32. Death Grip

> Golf is fraught with symbolic death and, in response to it, we often become anxious and ready to grab.—Richard Keefe

Sam Snead is often quoted for his grip pressure metaphor: imagine you are holding a baby bird. Don't hold it so tight that you crush it; don't hold it so loose that it flies away. You'd be hard pressed to find golf instruction that recommends a tight grip. Yet it is obvious that our grips tighten the more pressure and tension we bring to our games. Have you ever wondered why this is? The answer seems to come from our evolutionary past. "Since we were arboreal primates swinging on vines, it is a natural and sudden tendency to respond to any threat to our survival by grasping onto something." Here again, we see how responses that helped our ancestors to survive are now activated by perceived threats to our ego. If no threat is perceived, there would be no need for excessive grip. Our challenge here, again, is to uncouple our self-value from the results of our golf game.

Since we no longer swing from trees, another modern-day equivalent of the death grip is the tendency to brake through a curve. I was driving recently with snow on the ground, and as my truck started to slide in the turn the "death grip" tendency took hold for a moment as I went to apply the brake. But doing so would put the vehicle further out of control. The right approach is to not brake but to steer your way through the turn. This requires trusting physics, just as we need to trust physics with our golf swing.

Closely linked to the death grip is our misguided understanding of effort. In golf it is axiomatic that "less is more." We don't muscle a swing. Speed is produced by a fluid and relaxed swinging motion that occurs in a well-timed rhythm. If a fluid and relaxed drive goes 250 yards, it does not follow that swinging harder will send the ball 270 yards. Likely, that effort will result in topping or slicing. While muscular strength can be an asset for a golfer, our best swing is not the result of muscular force. It seems paradoxical to consider that effort won't work here because it does in so many other situations. It seems counterintuitive to let the unconscious brain along with the club do the work. If you felt as if you're life was on the line, however, your threat protection system might want to step in to control the situation—and if you over grip the club then you are perceiving some kind of threat.

Notice what else is happening in your body when you death grip. Is your jaw clenched? Is there muscle tension in your shoulders and neck? Are you feeling a squeeze in your gut? Grip pressure is a very important aspect of *feel* and crucial to your swing's timing. Remind yourself that your life is not on the line. Practice holding the club with the right amount of grip pressure—through all phases of the swing.

33. Set Up and Shut Up (or If You Think; You'll Stink)

> The golfing area of the brain is a fragile thing that is terribly susceptible to suggestion. Golfers are gullible.—Harvey Penick

Thinking is incompatible with optimal performance. Self-consciousness is an obstacle in golf, and every other sport. We may require conscious thoughts to get us into the position to perform our best but, once we have used the thoughts to "set-up," we must then learn to "shut-up."

Carl Hiassen affirms: If I'd learned anything about my golf game ... it was this: "The longer I stare at the ball, the more likely I am to botch the shot. So I made the radical decision to take my brain out of the process—a strategy that I highly recommend. With uncharacteristic resolve and no cognitive activity whatsoever, I stepped up to the putt and sank it for the win." What Hiaasen means is that he had no conscious, deliberative, prefrontal cortex brain activity (of course there was activity in his frontal lobes, he just couldn't notice it). Instead, he allowed the motor area of his brain—that knows how to stroke a short putt—to do what it knows how to do. He successfully got "out of his own way." This example shows anyone can do this, even without training. Training, of course, makes the possibility more available and thus more likely to be used.

Even with the best of intentions, thoughts may creep into our swing. If you are over the ball and notice the talk-space of the mind active, stop and step away from the ball. Take a mind FIT breath and readdress the ball.

The pre-shot routine can be likened to the process a pilot goes through before flying an airplane. The pilot goes through internal and external checklists. We as the golfer must do similar checks—wind, lie, moisture, distance, obstacles. The next check involves strategy—target, club selection, type of shot. Like the pilot, these checks provide the foundation for the successful golf shot. Once this foundation is set, the golfer can proceed without thinking to the actual shot—based on *feel*. A solid preparation foundation helps to establish a faith in *feel*, a trust that can cut through nerves, pressure, and adversity.

Don't stand over the ball too long allowing doubt to take root. Don't stand over the ball waiting for a feeling of readiness to arise. Execute a strong, consistent pre-shot ritual and stand over the ball ready to swing. Trust that you will make the swing you intend. We prepare for the shot and then execute the shot. If the Storytelling Mind is absent and the preparation is sound—that is, we have taken care to make proper alignment, posture, grip, and grip pressure—we will make our best shot.

Too much information during the swing can be a detriment; too many swing thoughts keep you in risky talk-space. Changing your swing in the middle of a round is likewise a detriment. It suggests a lack of faith in what you know. The solution is not technical—its *feeling*. At those moments, we need to move down into the body instead of up into the mind. If your swing is not working, pause. Take some mind FIT breaths and groove your swing slowly focusing on FI. This is not to say that we should never adjust or change our swing technique. Such changes can be beneficial and they take time to integrate. Trying to incorporate a new change into your swing in the middle of a round is likely to bring the swing more frontal—that is, talky—and less motor—that is, unconscious and grooved.

34. Your Wish is My Command

> I can airmail the golf ball, but sometimes I don't put the right address on it.—Jim Dent

The brain is like an information-processing machine. When we play, we are processing different kinds of information and programming our golf "computer." We can call this information *feel* and it is our intuitive ability to *read* what is happening and feel it in the body. When you putt you read the greens, judging your line and pace. This information gets programmed into the body that then knows—as if by magic—how to roll the putt. That is, if the Storytelling Mind doesn't get in the way. It is the same programmed *feel* that reads the distance to the green and executes the chip or pitch to get us on the green and as close to the pin as possible. The challenge is to trust our ability to do this and get out of the way once the inputs have been processed. It is not enough to exhort "trust yourself" or "commit to the shot." You need to have a methodology to build this trust. Mind Fitness provides this methodology by increasing the bandwidth of intuition— the recognition of embodied feelings.

Attention is not a boundless resource. We can expand our attention capacity through Mind Fitness training, but we must still allocate these resources under the severe conditions of selectivity discussed in Chapter 11. We can think of attention as computer RAM. The more RAM available, the more that can be processed in any given moment. Mind Fitness training is like a RAM upgrade.

The brain will try to obey the commands that we give it. It doesn't matter if these commands accurately reflect reality. The story of Mr. Poliwinkle demonstrates the unmitigated power of belief and how belief can lead to confidence. Belief can authorize superior performance by eliminating self-imposed obstacles, such as subtle muscle movements that go into steering putts. Mr. Polwinkle collected vintage golf clubs from erstwhile golf champions. His home library was replete with a magnificent collection. He only enjoyed these clubs as collectibles, never playing with them. However, one day he decides to swing the "Braid driver." Because the club belonged to that champion, Mr. Polwinkle reasoned so did the ability to swing the club as he did. Taking these clubs out of his library and into match play with his steady opponent Mr. Buffery, Mr. Polwinkle was inspired by confidence and gave him 18 strokes instead of the usual). Needless to say things did not go as planned. Mr. Polwinkle was down six with eight to play. By some circumstance, Mr. Polwinkle receives a wooden putter from another golfer, sent via caddy. The caddy reveals that the putter belonged to young Tom Morris. Buoyed by this belief, Mr. Polwinkle putted the lights out of the remaining holes and won 2 and 1, leaving Mr. Buffery stunned.

We've all perhaps noticed the transient improvement in performance that comes from a new club. It might be a feature of the club, but much of this improvement comes from the new FI information. Of course, along with this new information is a belief and confidence in the new club that allows us to relax and swing more naturally. We can become addicted to the quest for this fresh FI as was the case with Stephen.

Stephen had commitment issues. While in his personal life he had just gotten married, in his golf life he couldn't make a commitment to a putter. He was renowned for having over 100 putters in his collection. He'd switch when the putter he was using got "cold." He'd get a new putter and he would start to get "hot again." He would play this club until it, too, after a fashion, got cold. This cycle continued and his collection of putters grew. Perhaps he has Titleist, Ping, and Odyseey stock? I explained to him what might be happening here. Each time he changed the club it gave him a different feel—different weighting, different grip, etc. This new feeling helped him to connect to his FI for his putting stroke. Over time, these new feelings became habituated. This is what the brain is supposed to do—rotate constant information into the background of awareness so we can devote precious attention resources to new and potentially important information. His challenge was to keep the club "fresh" by focusing more on his FI. By rotating this information into awareness, it remains new; deliberate attention tells the brain, "Hey, this is important, stay awake." Stephen decided he wanted to make a long-term commitment to *one* putter. To pull off this "marriage," he would have to learn how to love this putter with caring attention; he would have to cultivate awareness of the dynamic moment-by-moment *feeling* of this instrument. The putter would need to become an extension of his mind and body. He did so and, over the course of the season, his putting improved and was more consistent. He remains happily married to his one putter and his wife!

35. Slice Virus

A virus is a self-replicating entity. Scientists debate whether they are living organisms. What can't be debated is the destructive power they hold. Some viruses, such as shingles, once a part of the host can never be eradicated. Drugs or the immune system can suppress them, but they may reappear at any time, especially under stress. Likewise, we can think of swing flaws as viruses. Our slice or hook or shank can never be fully eradicated. They may arise, likewise, under stress, when the mind is preoccupied or distracted or pressured.

It doesn't take much of a change to send a shot off into the woods or a water hazard. A miniscule change in the angle of the club head, a slight increase of speed at the top, or an alteration, however slight, in our swing mechanics, and, voila, we have a change in the path of the ball. 1/32 of an inch change in club face angle will send the ball 30 yards off path on a 300-yard drive. This happens to pros and duffers alike.

Shanking is such a dreaded prospect that some golfers, in superstitious fashion, won't even say it aloud. They'll refer to the "s-word." Superstitious or not, we will sometimes hit shots we don't intend, just as Jim Furyk did at the 2012 U.S. Open—a duck hook off the 16th tee cost him a tie for the lead and ultimately the tournament. Tour professionals hit balls into hazards with distressing regularity or is it comforting regularity for the golf viewing public?

People often get shingles after a stressful period in their life. Is stress causing your slice virus to emerge? If so, there are steps you can take to mitigate the impact of this strain. First, make sure you are committed to your pre-shot routines. Second, use your Mind Fitness techniques to bring your mind into the present moment. Stress suggests that the mind has been in the future—that is, worry—or the past—that is, regret—or in an obsessive commentary on the present (while these thoughts may refer to the present moment, they are not actually the experience of the present moment; they may be something like "Don't leave it short, a--hole."). Take a few body-based breaths to bring yourself back into the present. Repeat as necessary. Third, use the energy of the stress to enhance your performance. Fourth, check your swing mechanics. Are you too close in your stance? Has your grip pressure changed? Have you gotten quick at the top? Make any adjustments that are necessary. Do some of the exercises presented in the Appendix to help you re-establish connection to the relaxed FI for your swing. And, finally, see the viral swing as an anomaly. Don't allow thoughts to aggregate it into some kind of enduring pattern. Accept that it has happened, review the shot for any actionable feedback and then return to your next shot free from the last one. Don't allow it to cast a shadow over your next shot.

36. The Ultimate Shot

> It is nothing new or original to say that golf is played one stroke at a time. But it took me many years to realize it.—Bobby Jones

If there is a destination, we can be focused on getting there: Schenectady or bust. Along the way, we can be so focused on the goal that we miss what the ride has to offer—the scenery and the pure pleasure in the process of getting there. Golf, like life, is better considered a journey rather than a destination. We should really say golf "practice" rather than golf "game." Like psychotherapy, medicine, or law, golf is a continuous process of perfecting whatever it is we are doing when we are playing golf. Professional practices recognize that one never attains this perfection. We are always works-in-progress. Life is a practice, too. Mind Fitness is also considered a practice. One is never done.

Much of what we do comes in cycles. We never take one breath and are done breathing. We never eat one meal that lasts the rest of our lives (although it can sure seem that way at Thanksgiving). We never get that ultimate night of sleep. Golf, too, is a process that is never done. We have goals that can be either destinations or journeys. I want to be a scratch golfer. If I focus on the destination, I'm more likely to be frustrated at the non-linear progress that I make towards the goal. If I focus on process, I'll enjoy myself more along the way. I'll appreciate the beauty of the game; I'll marvel at the trajectory of a well-hit ball; I'll enjoy the amity of hours spent with friends and strangers playing this wonderful game.

Favoring results over process may be an old habit, so our minds will have to develop new habits and re-orient ourselves to the present moment where process happens. This takes practice. We'll inevitably move back and forth between focusing on the journey and the destination. While it might be the case that each golf shot moves us closer to becoming an expert, each golf shot is also a universe unto itself, a cycle with a beginning, middle, and end. Without expectations, agendas, or striving, this cycle can give us joy, no matter what happens.

37. Right Practice

> Work diligently, ardently, patiently, and persistently; you are bound to be successful, bound to be successful.—S. N. Goenka

We should practice in a way that develops confidence and recruits brain real estate for the skills we want. If you are impatient and unrealistic in practice, this is what you might get in your game. Go through your pre-shot routine before hitting a practice shot; hit sequences of shots rather than just pounding your driver through a bucket of balls—when does that ever happen on the course? Always aim. As Harvy Penick reminds us: "Aiming at something with your practice swing will help you learn to square the clubface. Never take another practice swing without aiming it at something."

Bill Clinton won the presidential election in 1992 with help from the slogan, "It's the economy, stupid!" For golf, we could substitute, "It's the short game, stupid!" Practice your short game. The full swing requires talent. For some of us, no amount of instruction or practice will result in 300-yard drives. For others, the right equipment, instruction, and practice can result in big swings. The great equalizer in golf is the short game. You don't need to be big, athletic, or strong to score. Many older golfers continue to score even as their full swing diminishes. The ego-driven golfer will spend more time on the egoic aspects of the game—driving in particular. Think of the adage: "Drive for show; putt for dough." And while driving is an essential part of the game, it tends to get a disproportional amount of attention. There is also more emphasis on distance over accuracy. Would you rather drive 280 into the second cut of rough—or the trees—or 250 in the fairway?

Practice training your mind and body as well as your swing. Golf requires all three to be prepared. Seek a personal trainer who specializes in golf or find resources through the Internet for golf-specific fitness. Many touring professionals run for fitness. Make your own routine. Mind Fitness training, ideally, could occur on a daily basis as well, and many activities that you do throughout your day can qualify as training. Formal Mind Fitness training is the premiere way to prepare and hone your mental skills. In addition, you can monitor yourself more informally through the day: Notice when the Storytelling Mind has become active and exercise your attention "muscle" to bring it back. Use your body training time to hone your concentration, making it fierce. Life itself can become one with our preparation for golf, and the benefits we derive from playing can feed back seamlessly into the rest of our life.

The following sets of suggestions frame a general approach to practice to promote long-term motivation. First, develop excitement and interest in a specific weakness of your game. Work with joy rather than dread to address this weakness. Second, be creative in how you approach it. Don't try to master golf all at once. Build on specific skills. For instance, work on holing 2 to 4-foot putts before you "expect" yourself to 2-putt every green you step on. Success is often aided by having a short-term memory lapse for failures. Third, we are best-served forgetting failure—once we have extracted any useful feedback from it and said "thank you"—and remembering success. Specifically, we want to remember the feeling of the successful swing so that we can invoke that FI the next time we swing. This is the case whether we are on the practice range, in an informal round, or a formal game. Four, have a plan for success and take responsibility for this plan. Set goals and work towards these goals. Evaluate your progress towards these goals with a compassionate eye and keep the feedback practical. In a matter-of-fact way, note any shortcomings and develop an action-based plan to get back on track. Avoid judging your value as a person on the basis of a lack of progress towards your goals. When self-judging happens, as it inevitably will, extricate yourself from this painful narrative and re-engage in the practical—that is, action-oriented—present.

Golf practice can be fun. Devise games that keep your interest engaged. For instance, you can practice getting up and down on a chipping green with a friend. For advanced players, David Cook presents a game that involves hitting nine key shots—low hook, normal hook, high hook, low straight, normal straight, high straight, low slice, normal slice, high slice. Play with a partner and have the partner call out the shot you need to make. You have five seconds to execute the shot. This type of practice helps to build confidence to hit any shot in any situation.

If you notice that practice, training, or even playing have become drudgery, stop. Look at your mind. What are you telling yourself? See if you can revise the story and re-engage with interest in what's happening in this very moment. Perhaps there is feedback in the situation that you can notice and integrate. Perhaps you are pushing too hard or not pushing hard enough. Perhaps you've lost the connection to your goals and purpose. Now would be a good time to reaffirm them. "What is my purpose?" can be a helpful question. Practice exquisite self-care, making sure you've eaten adequate and high-quality foods, are hydrated and well rested—both from sufficient sleep and time off from playing.

Don't be afraid to play up. If you find yourself always playing with partners whom you are superior to, check in on your ego-orientation. Playing with superior players can be a fabulous learning experience as long as we remain process-oriented. I routinely play with a younger friend who has to give me many strokes. We play every round as match play and—with credit to the handicap system—play rather evenly. He has a beautiful stroke that I watch with alacrity.

The recently emerging field of positive psychology reminds us that positive qualities of mind can and need to be cultivated deliberately. There are rare individuals who are naturally optimistic, but most of us have to work at it to some extent. Evolution provides us with a negativity bias. Since golf was not a selective pressure in the evolution of our species, this negativity bias will do nothing to improve our golf game. The FIT mind is a positive mind. This does not have to be Pollyanna but can be realistic optimism. It's as if we are pointing ourselves in the direction we would like to go and giving ourselves a gentle push in that direction. We can get there more efficiently with an encouraging word. Your great grandmother was right, you can get more flies, or in our case, more greens in regulation, with honey than vinegar.

38. Swing Like You Don't Care

> We become hostage to the accumulation of the 2s and 3s and 4s and 5s we covet, en route to the 70s, 80s or 90s we aim for to validate our golfing selves, that the point of the pencil begins to leach into our swings. Our arms grow heavy, our grips tighten. Our teeth clench. Our spirits sag ... and our numbers spike like a fever.—Jeff Silverman

There is sound wisdom in the advice above to avoid what Jeff Silverman termed "lead poisoning." Much suffering comes from attending to scoring in the way that he points out. But this is not the only way we can relate to scoring. What if we related to it without attachment? The outcome of our game is only a problem if we base our well-being on it. This is not required. Attention to scoring can be a precarious edge to walk. It is hard not to want more—or less, as is the case with golf. Yet, scoring is an indicator of *something*. Is it an indicator of success? What does the score mean for you? And why are you so attached to it? Will your spouse and dog love you less if you don't score? Is scoring all we care about?

When we show up for this shot prepared and FIT, we don't need to *care*. Care, in this sense, is infused with anxiety, a desire for an outcome that moves us away from the process that will actually get us there. When we show up for this moment with wholehearted attention, we can *act* without thinking. Our intention is impeccable and pure and matched with a readiness emerging from practice and commitment to routine. Attachment to an outcome is a sneaky disease that can flare-up at any moment. To be free of this disease we must bring FIT awareness to each shot. The price of this freedom is eternal vigilance.

Virtually every golf mental game coach encourages playing one shot a time. Golf is a game of independent events that are aggregated into holes and rounds and seasons. These categories have validity of course, but the shots that comprise them can also be seen as autonomous events—one shot does not necessarily have to influence the next. The more we can treat each shot as a singular event requiring our utmost attention, the better off we will be. If the future or the past is part of the landscape of the shot in front of you, then 100 percent of your attention can't be on the shot. Give up the past and stop chasing the future. Give yourself over to this shot. Rick Reilly quotes the pro Nick Price embracing the philosophy of one shot at a time—and for him, the associated beneficial results of winning the British Open, PGA, and seven other tour events. "For the first time in my life, I'm able to play each shot for its own value, its own worth. I'm playing each shot absolutely by itself, without anything attached to it, without thinking, 'OK, this is big, I've *got* to have this.' Or, 'I just bogeyed that last hole, I've got to hit this close.' Or, 'I need three birdies in a row here to win.' And I'm doing it whether it's a practice round or the last round of a major."

If we can give our wholehearted attention to each shot, as if we don't "care" about the results, then we are not allowing the past or future to influence this shot. It's not that we don't really care in the sense of being lackadaisical. On the contrary, we care so much that we are willing to give everything to this shot. And that brings us into the timeless and effortless present.

WISDOM

If the benefits of Mind Fitness only served us on the golf course, that would be a good thing. However, it's not hard to imagine these techniques, principles, and insights having a beneficial effect on the rest of our lives. It has almost become cliché to compare golf to life, but there is a core of wisdom to this chestnut. How we live our lives will come through in our game and, likewise, how we play our game will come through in our lives. A wonderful synergy can arise between the two. Out of this dynamic we can feel more connected to ourselves and the world around us. We can experience more significance in each moment. This is our life right now standing before us. We can bring a wholehearted devotion to hitting the golf ball that is before us and appreciating the life this golf swing lives within.

39. If You Aim at Your Target You've Already Missed

Traditional wisdom says: if you aim at your target you've already missed. To resolve this paradox, we need to look at the relationship between intention and effort. How can you hit the target if you don't aim, you might ask? Doesn't every instruction book, including *The Little Red Book*—the bestselling sports book of all time--encourage picking a target and aiming at it? Of course, it is necessary to take aim, but when we do so we may also bring striving to that aim. The aim needs to be free of desire. If we *need* to hit the target, that desire will interfere with the execution of the swing that get us to that target. Desire underlies almost everything we do in our game (and life). We desire to play our best, to score our best, to make pars and birdies. We desire to make a good impression on our playing partners and any other observers. The shot without *aim* is a pure shot. It abandons all such desires. It is *impeccable.*

The Zen teacher Shunryu Suzuki talks about burning through desire: "In order not to leave any traces, when you do something, you should do it with your whole body and mind; you should be concentrated on what you do. You should do it completely, like a good bonfire. You should not be a smoky fire. You should burn yourself completely. If you do not burn yourself completely, a trace of yourself will be left in what you do."

Self-conscious thinking eats up energy the way a plasma television eats up electricity (about the same as your refrigerator). At higher levels of the game, reductions in performance are usually the result of putting something in the way rather than something being missing. To be impeccable is to be prepared, pure, and effective. It is to have no excuses and nothing that gets in the way. It is to show up for this shot, this round, and this life.

Standing on the 17th tee box at Weston Golf Club, Todd Trono and I were looking at a downhill green 154 yards away. I was caddying for him to help him with his mental game. He took a seven iron and hit a knockdown shot. The ball whirred through the air like a steamer ship cutting through the ocean. One of our playing partners, noticing its trajectory, uttered some complimentary expletive. The shot headed straight to the pin took one bounce and dove into the cup. Watching his swing, I was struck by how *pure* it appeared. There was no extraneous movement: perfect balance, effortless effort, and impeccable timing. The swing also sounded *pure*. Thus, I coined it the *Pureland*. The *Pureland* shot is impeccable. Nothing is added, nothing is missing. It's a pure expression of the golf swing. Such swings don't happen frequently. Ben Hogan is famous for saying that he only hit a few shots each round as intended.

Mind Fitness helps us to get access to the *Pureland* through proper practice and instruction and execution in the moment. Golf is ideally suited for impeccability because we "control" so many of the factors. The ball is stationary. The ball will do, consistent with the laws of physics, what we "tell" it to do. In other words, the action of the ball follows directly from the action of the impact. Impeccability is an inner readiness born from giving up desire.

The classic *Zen in the Art of Archery* makes this point clear: "'The right art,' cried the Master, is purposeless, aimless! The more obstinately you try to learn how to shoot the arrow for the sake of hitting the goal, the less you will succeed in the one and the further the other will recede. What stands in your way is that you have a much too willful will. You think that what you do not do yourself does not happen."

40. The Antidote to Exhaustion is Not Necessarily Rest

We can become weary playing golf. Our scores don't improve as we hack away year after year. It can be exhausting. Our natural tendency when confronted with exhaustion is to seek rest; however, Brother David Stendl-

Rast suggests that the "antidote to exhaustion is not necessarily rest ... the antidote to exhaustion is wholeheartedness." This seems to be something of a contradiction: moving towards instead of away. Half-heartedness in life and golf may itself be the cause of exhaustion and is the opposite of Mind Fitness. When we are mind FIT we give everything we have to this moment. We don't hold anything back.

Can we bring this attitude of wholeheartedness to our golf game? After all, the four hours we devote to a round is our life in that moment—a big chunk of our day. We can spend those hours wrapped up in an agenda—those ideas, contingencies, and desires that determine whether we've had a good day or not. Or, we can endeavor to be fully present to whatever unfolds during that time—letting go of expectations and allowing ourselves to be surprised. These four or so hours are a time to enjoy the fellowship of friends, family, and strangers, to breathe fresh air, to participate in the sensory splendor of fairways, greens, ponds, and woods; a time to be with our bodies as they move in the very particular ways we ask them to move playing golf. When playing alone especially but even within a social round, much of the experience can be contemplation. Without agendas we are bound to enjoy the experience more.

Harvey Penick, in his *Little Red Book,* points to wholeheartedness when he speaks of aiming at a target. "Once you address the golf ball, hitting it has got to be the most important thing in your life at that moment. Shut out all thoughts other than picking out a target and taking dead aim at it."

Can we, on the one hand, take ourselves serious enough to treat this moment with full presence and, on the other hand, not get so serious about it? Seriousness often bleeds into moroseness and springs from the stories we tell ourselves. *Being* doesn't require stories. *Being* requires our wholehearted attention. We all have the capacity to be wholehearted. However, our capacity to do this at will or to do it routinely may need to be trained. We *know* how to do this. We all know how to *be*. It is very likely that you've had moments like this on the golf course and they may contribute to your passion for the game.

The actor Jack Lemmon tried and failed 34 times to make the cut at the Pebble Beach Pro-Am. He was not "successful" if you measure success in results, but he was successful in enjoying the process in a wholehearted manner. His persistence was testimony to the intrinsic value of having the opportunity to play golf and the seductive appeal of "this is going to be your year, Jack."

41. No Thank You

> What does golf allow me as a human being? It allows me to hate myself more than I already do in my daily life.—Lewis Black

When we allow other people's opinions or behavior, whether real or imagined, to affect us, we have given our power to the other. In a sense, we are saying to them: "Here, you hold this—my self-worth—and do with it what you will." They may drop it on the floor, neglect it, or treat it according to their whim. Meanwhile our feelings get yanked around, leaving us feeling bad and out of control. We can learn to say "no thank you" to the opinions of others. We can choose to be responsible for managing our own sense of self-worth and to make this self-worth non-contingent on events that we cannot control. When you think about it, isn't it a form of insanity to base our well-being on things that we cannot control?

If we are concerned about how we might appear to others on the golf course, we are giving away our self-worth. For example, if we get self-conscious about the pace of play and don't take time to do our pre-shot routine, we are allowing others to exert undue influence.

We can also give our self-worth away within ourselves. The mind produces all manner of thoughts, images, and feelings. It spins these mental contents into stories, beliefs, and expectations. Sometimes—too often, perhaps—this mind stuff is negative: judgmental, damning, critical. Even while the negativity is present, there is a quality of mind that can notice these contents. This observing mind is process-oriented and does not have to identify, that is, believe, what the mental contents say. If we don't believe them, we won't be swayed by them. When we don't buy into our own bad press, we have more opportunity to be calm, confident, and composed on the course. We don't have to hate ourselves.

One day I was walking downtown with my Rhodesian Ridgeback, Ruki. I remember that I was wearing a brightly colored, boldly patterned paisley shirt. We crossed the paths of three young people, teenagers probably. In this group of three was a girl, closest to us, and two boys. They were walking arm-in-arm. As they walked by, the girl reached out to touch my dog, and one of the boys said, "stupid faggot." I stared to get defensive: "How dare he say this ...", and so forth. Since I teach the lesson of non-reactivity to people all the time, I was able to catch myself in the midst of creating an ego-protecting narrative. First of all, was I certain he was addressing me? Perhaps he was addressing his companion. Assuming that he was addressing me, so what? He's entitled to his opinion and that's all that utterance is—his opinion. It has no power other than the power I bestow upon it. Why would I want to give my power away in this manner? I didn't want to, so I didn't. I laughed and moved on with my life in the moment. How often, though, are we giving our power away to a poorly struck wedge or a putt that lips out? I didn't buy into what this kid said about me, but when we get frustrated on the course, we are buying into what our own minds say about us. We believe the rants of the mind. Whenever one of our rules is violated, we are at risk for generating strong and thereby disruptive emotion. Instead of buying into the mind, we can thank it for the service of showing us where are prone to be reactive—in other words, where the buttons are and what can press them. Be wary of linking golf-performance and your worth as a human being. By bringing more awareness to these vulnerabilities, we can work on them in private without making a jackass of ourselves in public. No one shot, hole, or round can tell us much about what sort of golfer we are, let alone what sort of person we are. Ideally, we train our minds to respond to adversity with curiosity, asking ourselves, "What can this situation teach me?" Embrace the lesson, say "thank you," and move on. Nothing has to touch our core sense of self-worth; none of what happens on the golf course—nor anywhere else in life—need determine our self-value.

42. Thank You

> Overcoming adversity and learning from difficulty teach us about suffering ... They also pare down the special self, showing us that often we are not in control of our circumstances, but only (and imperfectly) of our own behavior. Reducing self-blame and keeping faith in ourselves when everything seems to be going against our wishes or desires will allow us to climb out of the self-esteem trap.—Polly Young-Eisendrath

Turning adversity into advantage would be a nice little coup. Mind Fitness allows us to do this. If we can come to any situation without our self-esteem on our sleeves, we can be open to what the moment has to teach us, whether this is an occasion to celebrate or a time to reflect on a mistake. To accomplish this, we shift our focus from protecting our self-image to the actions of the moment. We can be critical of an action without condemning ourselves. We can be disappointed about an outcome without deflating ourselves. This attitude shift, of course, takes practice. Few of us can do it naturally, so we must cultivate this attitude, like practicing a virtue.

We nurture this virtue by having the following question foremost in our mind: "What can I learn here?" When we receive the answer to this question, in polite fashion, we say, "Thank you." Thank you captures the essence of gratitude, the virtue of gratitude. Neuroscientists and positive psychology researchers have discovered that faculties like gratitude, compassion, and optimism can be trained. The brain is very changeable—plastic—in this regard.

We can be grateful for the opportunity to play golf at all. We can be thankful that we have the health and ability to play, and the green earth to play upon. We can be appreciative of everything that went into the construction of this golf course—the sacrifices that animals and plants made, and the labors of humans, earthworms, and bees. By cultivating gratitude, we don't take things for granted, we don't go to sleep and miss out on life in the moment.

Gratitude practice may seem counterintuitive: "You mean I'm supposed to say *thank you* when I shank my drive into the hazard?" Yes, this is exactly what I mean. Such gratitude is an antidote to anger and frustration. "Elite athletes tend to be quite passionate about their failures." By doing so, they can approach failure as a learning experience.

They can say, "Thank you!" to adversity because adversity is a potent teacher. They seek to integrate the feedback from the failure to improve future performance. They don't get caught up in protecting their ego. They don't spin stories of shame in response to the failure. Their "self" is not on the line, and therefore not at risk from the setback. They don't get frustrated, angry, or discouraged because they can maintain an attitude of gratitude towards the present moment. When negative emotions are present, they point in the direction of ego-involvement—that's the bad news. The good news is that their presence provides an opportunity to acknowledge them and then disentangle ourselves from ego-orientation back to the process-orientation of the present moment.

We can understand the importance of gratitude further by examining confidence. If we think of confidence as our ability to perform well at a task, with certainty, repeatedly over time, then we can distinguish self-efficacy from self-esteem. Self-esteem refers to self-worth and it is dangerous when one's self-value gets entangled in something as unforgiving as golf. Self-efficacy refers to the skills and abilities that we have and the opportunities that we enjoy. To the extent that these abilities don't become the basis of self-worth, we can maintain our sanity and our motivation to play, even when things are not going well. We can always work to have more effectiveness without worrying about worthiness.

43. Then They Still Have You in Prison

Two Vietnam War veterans and prisoners of war meet each other for the first time since their captivity. The first vet has undergone a process of self-exploration and has practiced forgiveness towards his captors. By doing so, he has been able to move on with his life and work with his post-traumatic stress disorder. He asks his compatriot if he has likewise undergone a process of forgiveness. The second vet looks incredulously at the first as if he didn't hear him correctly: "What? Are you kidding me? I'll never forgive them? How could you even suggest that?" The first vet sighs and notes with a touch of sadness, "Then they still have you in prison, my friend."

Forgiveness is an emerging field in psychology that recognizes the detrimental health consequences of holding a grudge. Research has shown that being in a state of unforgiveness can elevate stress hormones such as cortisol in a way that is consistent with chronic stress overload. Researchers at Stanford have developed an intervention that helps people forgive whether this is forgiving another, an institution, god, or oneself. This approach to forgiveness is mostly an internal affair. We seek to re-orient ourselves to the present and away from the painful narrative about a past event.

It's quite possible—on smaller scale—that we are in one state of unforgiveness or another with ourselves when we play golf. Each missed shot is an occasion for beating ourselves us, holding a grudge—even against our "offending" clubs—and, no doubt, elevating our stress hormones. We might even rue the day we took up golf. It's not a joke that we might treat ourselves without mercy. Like the Vietnam veteran cited above, we carry around our past: the 3-putt on 7, the out-of-bounds drive on 13, the chunked chip on 18. These accumulated injuries add up and take a lot of energy. It's like carrying around a big sack of stones on our shoulders. Each unforgiven action goes into the bag and we just mindlessly carry it around. Think how much lighter we would feel if we could empty things out of this sack or, better yet, chuck the entire thing. This is what we do in any moment we are fully present. The bag of accumulated sorrows can only exist with reference to the past. Let it go.

44. Watching the Grass Grow

It was one of those backed up Saturdays at my old home course. The front nine on this par 60 can get congested. I was playing alone and another single caught me around the 4th hole as I was waiting to tee off. We agreed to play together. The next hole, another single caught us and joined our twosome. He was in a hurry and, as we were approaching the green on 6, he saw that the tee box on 8 was open. He begged out and continued on his way. As we sat on the tee box of 7 waiting and watching the group ahead of us lollygagging, we decided to make a break for the 8th tee. As fortune would have it, the slow group ahead of us on 7 finally finished up and was also heading over to the 8th tee at the same time. When we collided, we politely asked if they minded if we played through, as etiquette would dictate. To our surprise we got the following response: "No. You don't play through on this short course." When we pointed out that they were backing things up, they denied it and pointed to the person who just teed off on 8. We clarified that he had been playing with us and skipped ahead. Their spokesperson went on to say, "If you don't have patience you shouldn't be out here playing." Hmmm. Interesting. If patience is key, then "surely your group wouldn't mind waiting for a few minutes as we played through," I thought to myself. To my later astonishment, the spokesperson was not some Sunday golfer, but was a member of the course.

Of course, we should play with patience and enjoy the game on a breezy Saturday afternoon. We should also be mindful of others on the course and observe golf etiquette. When the course is backed up, the course is backed up. There is nowhere to go, so enjoy the ride. Making the decision to play through versus play back can be confusing. I liken it to being cold. If you are cold and sitting by an open window that is easily accessible, get up and close the window. There is no particular virtue in shivering if you have it within your means to make a change. However, if there is no window to close, then we must accept the cold and work with it. On the course, we should avoid becoming frustrated with the group ahead of us. If you want to play faster and can play through, play through. If you cannot, accept what is happening in the moment. Avoid generating judgmental tales critical of the hapless or selfish souls playing ahead. If no one is coming up behind me, I take advantage of these situations to play multiple balls and practicing chipping and putting.

Mind Fitness can be a benefit in these situations because it provides a permanent cure for boredom, restlessness, and impatience. Any situation that might have been associated with these vexations in the past, such as being stuck waiting for someone, can now be an opportunity for Mind Fitness training. Beyond this boredom antidote, Mind Fitness helps us to be exquisitely interested in what is happening now, even if this is watching the grass grow.

45. Equanimi-Tee

> Equanimity is a radical permission to feel your feelings all the way through and a willingness to fully experience what is taking place in our senses and our feelings before acting.—Polly Young-Eisendrath

Deepak Chopra was inspired to write *Golf for Enlightenment: Seven Lessons for the Game of Life* a mere six months after playing his first round of golf. As Rick Reilly describes in humorous fashion in *Whose Your Caddy?,* playing golf is the supreme test of enlightenment. As Reilly caddies Chopra, the bestselling author and wellness guru reveals his humanity. No disrespect is meant towards Dr. Chopra, for who hasn't felt the sting of self-importance on the course? Nonetheless, Chopra's on-course antics are ironic to say the least and reveal an important facet of self-development. Skills are one thing; application of skills is another. It is one thing to have a working understanding of equanimity. It is another to execute this learned skill. Equanimity is a choice we must make in any given moment. Reilly reveals this tidbit on Chopra's game: "He butchered No. 4, unleashing a few swear words along the way. You just don't expect to hear a man of infinite peace, a man who has lifted himself above worldly desires and avoidances, a man who has freed himself from ego and envy, say 'Goddamn piece of shit' under his breath."

Let's consider equanimity. My online dictionary offers the following definition: "mental calmness, composure, and evenness of temper, especially in a difficult situation." And then lists the timely example, "She accepted the good and the bad shot with equanimity." We can add to this definition the notion of *interest*—being curious about what is happening. If we bring interest to a situation, our mind is open—we are not beating ourselves up, bemoaning our fate, getting bent of shape. Interest leads to acceptance.

Reilly is skeptical of Chopra and, having read his books on healing, he muses, "Golf just doesn't usually give a rat's ass about the 'infinite organizing power of your cells,' does it? Golf just wants to yank down your pants in front of the Ladies Senior Auxiliary Luncheon and slap you in the face a few times." Reilly continues with another tidbit: "And then on the 7th tee box, a par 5, he drilled more skulls than a neurosurgeon. He topped one, two, three straight drives into some nasty weeds. At this point he didn't look like a guy playing the front nine at the Garden of Eden." Chopra's golf pro, Wendy Werly chides him to reflect on what he is doing, and he realizes that he is not "breathing." He also succumbs to negative swing thoughts on the 8th tee box. "I must not slice here. I dream about slicing here, it torments me."

I might view Chopra as a phony, if I hadn't succumbed to all the same emotions myself. This is the beautiful singularity of golf. It is the supreme challenge. There is nowhere to hide. The ball does not lie in where it lies. It shows anyone who plays the boundaries of their ego. It shows me, at every turn, where I am still reactive, protecting myself from imaginary injuries. With every bad reaction, there is an opportunity to let go and get closer to equanimity. Insight alone is usually not sufficient. We still have to make the choice to do something differently. We still have to remind ourselves to breathe in difficult circumstances, no matter how long we've been practicing, no matter how much self-awareness we have, and no matter how spiritual we believe ourselves to be. No one is immune, not even a man of *infinite peace*.

Equanimity is our ability to engage any circumstance with an interested and matter-of-fact attention. Getting nervous in response to seeing a hazard is not equanimity on the golf course or what we might call: *equanimi-tee*. The hazard, if seen as a threat, will activate our threat response systems. If, instead, the hazard is treated as just another feature of the environment, we may have a better chance of not hitting into it. The spot you want to hit to is more relevant, anyway than the hazard. The hazard may inform club choice, if you need so much club to carry the water, but that is the only good information it offers. Our job is to stay connected to FI and enjoy the rhythm of the shot that will follow.

46. Be Thine Own Caddy

> If you want to feel self-confident, you have to face and overcome difficulties. In so doing you will learn how to work with yourself and others, and you will develop empathy and compassion for human suffering—a priceless insight.—Polly Young-Eisendrath

If you spoke aloud every self-referencing thought you had during a round of golf as if you were caddying for another player, you'd probably be out of a job. It's likely you wouldn't treat a dog the way you treat yourself. Would you call someone a "f---ing idiot"? Would you grind your teeth and snarl: "What the hell's wrong with you?" It's remarkable that we feel comfortable beating ourselves up in a way that we'd never treat another person. We give ourselves permission to berate ourselves when decorum, good sense, and compassion would prevent us from doing this to someone else.

While it may seem that the issue is that we hate ourselves in these moments of self-battery, I think it's more accurate to say that we are too self-preoccupied. In other words, this lack of compassion stems from an overemphasis on self-importance. We are taking ourselves too seriously, placing mortal significance on golf shots and golf scores. If this form of self-importance is showing up on the golf course, it is likely showing up in other areas of life. Recognizing how self-importance we are is an important first step in developing self-compassion. It's hard to feel compassion—which literally means *feeling pain together*—when we are so caught up in self-importance.

To get out of self-importance and into compassion, imagine that you are your own caddy. Treat yourself with the decorum and respect that you would afford a friend or even a stranger for whom you were looping. Don't let any self-talk go unchallenged that you wouldn't say aloud to someone you liked and respected. When you notice this self-talk arising—as it will continue to do because it is so deeply conditioned—ask yourself what seems so important? What's the agenda? For instance, it may be the agenda for "perfection" that is driving the self-judgment. Instead, can you give yourself some encouragement? When I catch myself self-flagellating and can let go, I might say: "C'mon Arnie ... " It's a moment of tenderness that hasn't lost sight of the goal of playing well. I'm able to let go, give myself permission to be imperfect. I may not play any better—who knows—but I will feel better about myself. I'm certainly not going to play worse.

47. Sweat When You're Hot; Shiver When You're Cold; Shank When You're Tense

No one is immune from the conditions—the rain falls on everyone, the horn blows for everyone, the heat bakes everyone, and the wind whips at everyone in the same way. The elements are the same; our reactions are individual. When it is cold, we will be cold; when it is hot, we will be hot. If you are on the 14th tee and it is a cold and rainy day, you can't just close the window. Cold is the condition of now and shivering discomfort may be a feature of this now. However, this is not usually the end of the story. We usually add quite a bit of self-talk to the physical conditions of now. We might take the conditions personally and feel threatened by them. Physical discomfort can become mental discomfort. We might become distressed and frustrated. While it's possible to play well under harsh external conditions, it's unlikely we'll play well when the internal conditions are also uncomfortable.

We can take precautions to protect ourselves from cold and rain with proper gear, but we can't do much about heat. We can take refuge in an air-conditioned clubhouse, but once we are out on the course, we will be hot on hot days. Our bodies will sweat. This, again, could be the end of the story, but usually it is not if we kvetch and complain and fuss about the heat. We might allow it to irritate us. Alternatively, we can accept what is so. By accepting what is so, we create a space around us that helps us to avoid distress. Sweating is inevitable; suffering is optional. Accepting the heat was the case the first time that I broke 100, I was playing in North Carolina summer heat and not in my comfortable and cool Vermont. It was close to 100 degrees and humid. I was walking the course carrying my clubs. It was too hot to swing hard—a fact that allowed me to get into the best swing rhythm I'd experienced to date. Needing to conserve my energy helped me to play better. I could not afford to be overly aggressive.

On that hot summer day, I was acceptance-in-action. So was Phil Mickeleson when he won the Buick Invitational at Torrey Pines after a bout of food poisoning. "I was too weak to have expectations," he said. When we don't accept, we are in resistance. In each moment, we have this choice: accept or not. The acceptance option enlarges our sense of possibility to include whatever is occurring in the moment. We don't create an opposition between our self and the conditions of the moment. We stick with the primary agenda of making our shot. The resistance alternative wastes energy and uses up the precious bandwidth of attention by focusing on the conditions we are complaining about. Whatever the moment brings, we can make the acceptance choice whatever the conditions: wind, rain, cold, humidity, bugs, hunger, thirst, tiredness, discomfort, or pain. Nothing can touch us.

48. The Great (Golf) Way is Not Difficult for Those Who Have No Preferences

> We are human beings that take form through an impetus to joy, interest, and concern.—Arnie Kozak

To give up all our preferences as the above epigraph suggests seems ludicrous. Why would we want to do such a thing? What possible benefit might it have? Wouldn't we become zombies if we had no preferences—aimless, apathetic, and unmotivated? Rather than giving up preferences, let's think about giving up our *attachment* to preferences. We'd like things to be a particular way, but we don't get distressed when they are not. Letting go of attachments clears the way to joy. Whatever happens is interesting. In a sense, we become like young children who find the world a ceaseless source of fascination.

By setting aside preferences we can shift from human *doings* to human *beings*. If we can come to our golf game as a human being, the game itself becomes a process of self-development, even spiritual development. If we are developing spiritually, golf becomes a refinement of and expression of our purpose. This certainly makes the time spent, greens fees, and membership dues more worthwhile. A radical freedom opens up in this space because, no matter what happens, we get value from the experience. A bumper sticker reads, "the worst day of golf beats the best day at the office." Of course, we can find value in our day at the office, too, when we invoke the philosophy of no preferences, but we'd still rather be golfing!

49. April Moon

> Humans are often at their best -- physically, emotionally socially, and spiritually—when engaged in non-threatening interactions with nature.—George W. Burns

To say it is orange is not right. Red-orange, perhaps. Blood-orange. The sun moved out of sight in the west just beyond the shoulder of the 18th tee box. As I turned my back to the burning star, I beheld the view from 18: The Green Mountains in their purple-mountain majesty, still snow-capped in April and littered with people earlier in the day carving lines through their snowy depths. I love the view from hole 18 at the Links at Lang Farm. Classic Vermont. Yet tonight there was something else. The moon in its full flower was rising just to the north of Bolton Mountain. This was certainly worth the walk around the course, certainly worth working through the fatigue and the soreness to continue playing this early season round (I had been one of those people carving lines on the mountain earlier in the day). As I hit my approach shot, it soared into the sky towards that fat moon. It was as if the moon blessed it and the shot rolled inside the edge of the green. We were able to finish in the waning light of the day. A summer day in spring and the close to a long winter, six months long.

The game of golf is played on one of the largest playing fields of any sport. We get to walk along the surface of the earth, chasing a tiny white ball. We are outside breathing fresh air. Even though this is a semi-natural world, we are enjoying a connection to the environment that has otherwise become a rarity in contemporary life.

The golf course is a special place that represents the union of nature and humanity. The great blue herons at my local course don't seem to mind that golfers surround the wetlands running through the course. The ground hogs, rabbits, and foxes don't seem to mind that their habitat has another purpose. Whatever your politics on the use of land for golf courses, it is certainly preferable to housing developments, which might often be the alternative to a golf course. There, the birds and animals may mind.

50. The Sharp Edge of a Razor is Difficult to Pass Over; Thus, The Wise Say the Path to Salvation is Hard

Training the mind and playing golf are difficult paths. Experienced meditation masters struggle with the mind and Tour professionals struggle with their game. No one is on his or her game all the time. If enlightenment was easy and golf consistent, we'd see Buddhas on every street corner and scores going lower and lower.

The word enlightenment carries a lot of cultural baggage and may conjure colorful notions for you. There are different kinds of enlightenment too. The type of enlightenment closely related to Mind Fitness does not entail a fireworks pageant of bliss and joy—although training the mind may be accompanied by bliss and joy. This enlightenment, which might better be called awakening, doesn't reflect a permanent transition. If you saw the 1946 movie *The Razor's Edge,* you saw a portrayal of enlightenment that feeds into cultural stereotypes. The main character, Larry Daryl, descends from his Himalayan mountaintop retreat displaying a luminescent glow. He speaks of having touched god.

Awakening can be far more ordinary. It can be far more accessible. You don't have to trek to the Himalayas to taste it. Awakening is here in any given moment and it can be enjoyed right here on the golf course. A simple definition of awakening: a moment of being aware that is unadulterated—no self-talking, no resistance, no wanting things to be other than they actually are. We can think of it as the quality of being when we are in full contact with what is happening now. This moment will pass, no doubt. If we practice the techniques in this book assiduously, we might be able to enter this state more frequently. We might be able to get out of our own way with more ease, especially when we are playing.

51. The Perfect Doubt

> Let's not take doubts with exaggerated seriousness, or let them grow out of proportion, so that we become black-and-white or fanatical about them. What we need to learn is how slowly to change our culturally conditioned and passionate involvement with doubt into a free, humorous, and compassionate one. This means giving doubts time, and giving ourselves time to find an answer to our questions that are not merely intellectual or "philosophical" but living and real and genuine and workable.—Sogyal Rinpoche

Doubts will inevitably arise in the process of developing as a golfer. No one can play such a challenging and frustrating game without the specter of doubt. We can get discouraged by these doubts or greet them with an openness. Doubt can remind us that we are alive and working to get better at a supremely difficult and rewarding game. Doubt suggests that our soul is involved in what we are doing. A fit mind can help us to deal with doubts as they arise.

The perfect doubt is loving the uncertainty of the moment, leaning into it, and embracing it with curiosity rather than fear. The perfect doubt is an antidote to pride and arrogance. It's not self-doubt, second-guessing, or lack of commitment. The perfect doubt is the basis for action. This doubt appreciates change, complexity, and variability with a smile.

52. Opening the Gate

When, exactly, does playing golf begin? Is it when we put on our shoes? Is it when we pick up a club to tee off? Is it when the first ball is struck? Ritual is a way of marking intentions. Rituals can be found in every human culture across time. Yet, rituals are also found in animals so there must be something biological about them. Rituals, no doubt, have had evolutionary significance for humans as well as nonhuman animals.

Rituals are often used in religious settings to facilitate a connection to the divine. Rituals help to create a sense of reverence and awe. The rhythmic nature of many religious rituals, such as chanting, drumming, and movement, trigger a deep relaxation response in the autonomic nervous system. Taken to an extreme this can trigger a process within the brain that breaks down our usual sense of boundaries between self and the world. If you have ever had a deep sense of connectedness while playing golf, it may stem from this type of brain activation. Whatever your religion, rituals can help you to establish a sense of dignity and respect for your golf game. Ritual will help you express your intention to play golf and to do so to the best of your ability.

How often, though, do we go through the motions during a round of golf? How often are we waling around as if obscured in a cloud of talking to ourselves about our last shot or worrying about the how we are going to pull off the next one? What if, instead, we treated each shot as a sacred act?

The pre-shot ritual will help to activate the brain and our intentions in a beneficial way. The value found in the rhythmic nature of many rituals is why, perhaps, the waggle is such a common pre-shot routine. It tells the emotional brain to pay attention and to provide the attention and energy to what is about to come. It helps us to get out of the Storytelling Mind and into the moment of action.

53. Take Off Your Shoes

In the poem "Fire in the Earth," David Whyte speaks of Moses receiving the command to "take off his shoes" as he approached the burning bush. This act of humility brought him closer to the earth, to the ground, and we learn that he "never recovered/his complicated way of loving again," and that "every step he took/from there was carefully placed." This image provides an invitation to approach our game with reverence and likewise humility. It invites us to treat each shot as sacred, to step on the green as if stepping into a holy place of worship. And we can partake of this worship regardless of our religious or spiritual beliefs. Each place on the course can become the "church" of golf, and this church knows no denominations and requires no dogmatic beliefs. It is open to anyone who wants to play. Treating golf with sacredness can help us to move closer to the divine in our lives, however that divinity is experienced. The divine can be manifest in nature, in ideas, or in the God of your choosing.

54. 54

> I have somehow tried to teach each of my students that golf and life are similar. There's nothing guaranteed to be fair in either golf or life, and we shouldn't expect it to be different. You must accept your triumphs and disappointments equally.—Harvey Penick

It has almost become cliché to view golf as a metaphor for life. Nevertheless, this comparison is fertile territory. Golf can be both the influenced and the influencer. Golf will reveal who we are and where we are in any given moment. Golf reveals character: How we approach golf is the way we approach life; how we approach life is how we'll approach our golf game.

Harvey Penick advocates a minimalist approach to the golf swing, and to golf in general. We can take this approach in life, too. At the end of the day, what makes a good golf swing is not technical information. It is the ability to integrate sufficient swing information into *feeling-image*.

To date, the record posted score for a PGA Tour event is 59, and this has been accomplished a handful of times on the PGA and once on the LPGA. Perhaps it is good that golf's holy grail is so unobtainable. It gives us something strive for and something to maintain our sense of awe. If someone shot a 54, would this open the way to inconceivable lower scores just as Roger Bannister breaking the 4:00 minute mile opened the way to lower times? Perhaps the pursuit of perfection is more gratifying than actually attaining it. With profound respect, we submit to the quest of 54. May we do so with a deep sense of gratification. May we do so with a profound sense of wonder. And for those few moments in the occasional round when we are playing as if we could shoot a 54, may we enjoy it while it lasts!

AFTERWORD

I hope these brief chapters provide the tools for changing your game and changing your life. It is my sincere intention that you find the wisdom contained in these pages practical so you can integrate it into your golf game and daily life. I am reminded of the poet Rilke when he said in his *Letters to a Young Poet*"You are so young, so much before all beginning, and I would like to beg you, dear Sir, as well as I can, to have patience with everything unresolved in your heart and to try to love the questions themselves as if they were locked rooms or books written in a very foreign language. Don't search for the answers, which could not be given to you now, because you would not be able to live them. And the point is, to live everything. Live the questions now. Perhaps then, someday far in the future, you will gradually, without even noticing it, live your way into the answer." We can love the questions of golf too.

We can think of Mind Fitness as a form of etiquette for the mind. The wisdom contained in this book can be considered, as one of my students said, "Emily Post" for the mind. Instead of etiquette as an external code of conduct designed to promote conformity, it can be viewed from the perspective of the golden rule. How would I want to be treated in this circumstance? In this way, etiquette is a path of practicing what is skillful.

We might think of wisdom as a process that develops out of how we relate to the experiences in our lives. Importantly: how we learn from adversity. Acceptance helps us to be resilient in the face of disappointment, pain, and other difficulties. Golf develops wisdom by helping us to relate to adversity in precisely this accepting and resilient way.

APPENDIX

The appendix contain practical exercises for developing Mind Fitness. By making these exercises part of your training routine, you will integrate the principles that have been presented here. The array of practices will give you an opportunity to find the ones that work best for you and to stick with them, making them part of your daily routine.

Overview: Mind Fitness Practices

Mind Fitness training has several themes. The first theme demonstrates how the mind can generate positive experiences. We are self-aware creatures who can influence the state of our minds. If negative thoughts are present, we can—by choice—aim for positive thinking. This is the plastic power of mind. The second theme focuses on observation of the mind without attempting to influence or control—in other words: Acceptance. Here we can pay attention to the subjective components of mind: feel, image, and talk. The third theme moves us into the objective *now* by orienting the mind to the senses of sight, sound, and bodily "touch" sensations. Grounding awareness in the senses is always available and a timely antidote to excessive activity in talk space and unlike grounding your club in a hazard, does not incur a penalty. The fourth theme focuses the mind on "rest" which is the pleasant sensation of relaxation in the body. We can find these pleasurable feelings even when we are "tense" or when parts of the body are in pain. The fifth and final theme is to focus on change. The mind and the senses are constantly changing: Self-talk gets loud and then quiets, images come and go, feelings wax and wane. We can pay keen attention to how and when things change, especially as things expand and contract. Together, these themes represent a comprehensive mind fitness-training program. Practicing them can build concentration, enhance our connection to the world of perception, and help us to have equanimity on the golf course. Each aspect of the mind is trained, much as you would go around a Cybex circuit training different muscle groups to achieve total fitness. A swing that starts wrong usually goes wrong from there. Many players compensate for bad technique, but let's try to develop excellent FI from the ground up. As with any practice, only good practice will lead to improvement. The motions you'll be grooving need to be verified on the course and checked with your swing instruction professional to make sure you are on course.

Theme One: Focus on The Positive

In the first theme, we orient the mind to something pleasant and positive. This could be a word of encouragement, an image of success, or pleasant feeling in the body—or a combination of these. We can tap into the power of the mind to generate the positive. Spend a few moments connecting to this positive, and *pleasant,* sense of your game. This positive sense is always present (see Theme Four below). We can choose to shift any negative feeling towards a positive one through our intentions. As a resource, create a list of positive memories of golf. You can remember a particularly pure shot, a great round, a fun round, a round when you appreciated beauty on the course, or felt at peace. Your pleasant memories don't have to be golf related. You can focus on anything positive and this will bring the benefits of positive thinking to you. Remember that you can come back to this affirmative place whenever you choose.

Theme Two: Acceptance

In the second theme, we use mental labeling to move us towards acceptance. When unpleasant or unexpected experiences arise during the course of our game, the FIT mind can treat these experiences analytically—*what mind space does this occur within?*— instead of getting swept along by the storyline of the misfortunes. There is noting: *fear, tension, memory, anticipation,* et cetera. This naming helps to contain the damage that may have resulted from reacting emotionally to whatever just happened. Remember that the mind's principle activity is talk. In any given moment, it can be talkative or quiet. When it's talking what it says can be helpful, harmful or neutral. You can also notice whether mental images are present. Likewise, in any given moment, there can be images in the mind or not (with or without talk). These, too, can be simply noticed. As well, feelings with an emotional flavor can be present to one degree or another (with or without talk and images). These can be labeled as "feeling"—or a quick reference to the feeling itself "anger"—without getting caught in the reasons for the anxiety. We just give it a quick name and move on. Labeling helps to create some distance from the experience, lessening its impact. Labeling leads to acceptance—a description of what is happening in the mind right now.

Theme Three: Ground Attention in the Present

All of the practices presented below—Standing, Seated, Body Scan, Walking, and others— develop the minds' capacity to be present—something we want to keep close at hand when we are golfing. The present mind is a FIT mind.

Theme Four: Find Peace in the Midst of the Storm

When things are going poorly, we need to have strategies to cope with the challenge. All of the Mind Fitness methods can be helpful in this regard and, more specifically, we can direct our attention to some positive aspect in any situation. If the body is tense and full of pain, we can find some part of the body that feels restful or peaceful. If our game has deteriorated and has become frustrating, we can focus on some aspect that is fluid without frustration. The first three themes provide the skills to make this transition to the restful aspects of experience "on demand." Awareness of breathing can help you to locate or even to create a restful place in the body. If you are having difficulty finding rest in the body, scan it with your attention and imagine your breath going to any part that feels tense. As you breathe, imagine the air opening this space and making it feel more peaceful.

Theme Five: Ride the Wave of Change

As we've seen in the 54 chapters of *Swing Like You Don't Care*, playing golf gives us access to wisdom. Golf shows us the changing nature of things. When we "get" this in our mind right down to our bones, we can handle whatever challenge comes our way. When you expect change, you won't be surprised when unexpected things occur. When you understand that variability is the rule, you won't cling to consistency.

MIND FIT PRACTICES

Seated

Your seated practice can be the incubator for all other practices. It can be the stronghold for Mind Fitness training and this foundation can be extended to briefer standing and walking practices.

To do this formal Mind Fitness practice, find a comfortable place to sit. Perhaps you can devote a small space in your home for doing this practice. There is no particular posture that you have to strike as long as it is comfortable and your spine is upright. Bring your attention to how your body feels in this moment, distinguishing between thoughts about the body and the actual physical sensations of the body. Pinpoint the location where you feel breathing sensations happening in the body—tip of the nose, mouth, chest—and direct your attention to this process without trying to alter it. Notice how these sensations change—arise and fade away; keep your attention with the energy rather than the idea of breathing. Whenever attention wanders into the future, the past, or talking about the present, bring it back to what breathing feels like now. We'll call this "taking your seat." When you sit down in your seat, confirm your intention to work with your mind. Be interested and open to what you'll find. See this interest as a way to enhance your golf game and your qualities as a human being.

The action of gently bringing attention back—from the future, past, or commentary—to your intended focus over and over again is the key action of Mind Fitness.

Imagery

Take five or ten minutes to establish your seat so that you are able to "catch and release" thoughts in the mind comfortably. Now you are ready to do some golf-specific practice. For example, if you are preparing for a particular round or match, you will use that match as the focus of your visualization. Alternatively, you may just want to visualize your home course with no particular tournament in mind. From your breathing seat, *picture* and *feel* each shot of an ideal round. As you sit in the formal practice seat, you'll feel the pleasure and satisfaction of this process. You'll feel relaxed and pleasurable sensations in the body. You are training your brain to play in the manner you imagine.

Relaxation, pleasure, and success will transfer from imagination to the golf course.

In addition to explicit rehearsal, you can also try developing symbolic imagery to augment other aspects of your game, such as mechanics. Develop an image that works for you. I have come to see my left shoulder as a mechanical and well-lubricated joint that is "affixed" in place by a steel trellis. This helps me to stay on plane. As I practice with this image, I am also cultivating the proper FI of the swing that is on plane.

Seated into Standing

Following your seated practice, move into your indoor practice area and take some golf swings. Swing from this place of relaxed pleasure that you generated in formal practice. As you swing, feel the whole swing as a fluid movement, almost like a dance. Then take note of your swing elements separately and in turn: weight shift, grip pressure, swing to balance, and so forth. This action lays the foundation for the FI. Do this practice for all your swings: driver, iron, wedge, and putting. Stay connected to breathing as you swing. You might want to inhale on the backswing and release the breath on the swing.

Standing

Start with a waggle, whether or not you use a waggle in your pre-shot routine. Use the waggle to find your stance. *Feel*—and see, preferably; do this practice in front of a mirror to get the visual corrective feedback—your feet making contact with the ground or the floor; get the *feel* of the correct stance, noting posture, position of the feet, bend of the knees and grip on the club. From this "grounding" waggle move into your backswing. Get to know the *feel* of the backswing and check its correctness. Make the back swing in an unhurried way. After four to ten iterations of waggle to back swing, take the full swing with full attention to body sensations. Keep your attention on the movement of the club and not any *talk* about your posture that may be arising. The club motion should be in the foreground of attention and the *feel* of the swing should be in the background.

You can do this exercise with a weighted swing trainer club. Doing so can help to accentuate the FI of your best swing. In addition, the weighted club helps to build swing-specific muscles.

Slow Motion Drill

Harvey Penick in his classic *Little Red Book* describes the slow-motion drill. The movement is *very* slow. By moving slow, we are laying down neural tracks in the brain; we are recruiting territory in the motor cortex for the swing. We are also developing the FI for the swing. Such slow-motion swinging can be—and should be—combined with mind FIT breathing. Penick recommends four repetitions of the partial swing—from the top down 1/3 of the way—followed by a slow full swing. Repeat this process over and over again. Harvey opines correctly: "Your golfing brain and your muscles learn just as well from repeating the swing in slow motion as from whapping away on the range. In fact, it can be higher quality learning because no mistakes are being made in the slow-motion swing."

Diaphragmatic Breathing

Once we can establish attention on natural breathing (in the way described in "Seated"), there are some advantages to learning how to breathe diaphragmatically. When the diaphragm is engaged, the belly appears to fill with air as the diaphragm moves south (the diaphragm is a wall of smooth muscle underneath the lungs). To figure out if you are breathing with the diaphragm, place one hand your chest and one hand on your belly. As you breathe, you should see the belly rising and falling but not your chest. This type of breathing is more efficient and activates the relaxing branch of the autonomic nervous system. The more you practice it, the more habitual it will become and the greater access to relaxation you'll enjoy.

Body Scan

The more familiar we are with what's happening in the body, the more access we'll have to FI. We want to be on intimate terms with the energy signatures of the body—sensations. We notice all the sensations, both pleasant and unpleasant with the same interest as if you were doing a geographical survey of the body. Body Scan Mind Fitness practice can be done in a formal, systematic way by conducting a guided tour of the body. An alternative to the systematic approach is to sit down or lie down and notice the most prominent sensations that are present in the body. Move attention to these sensations as they arise and fade away. When the mind becomes swept away by talk, bring attention back to the sensations present now.

Walking

Every time we walk is an opportunity to practice Mind Fitness. I encourage walking the course if this is possible for you. In addition to the exercise benefits this provides, it gives you plenty of time to practice WI-FI (walk-into-feel-image). Spend at least 100 yards per hole on long par 4s and 5s doing Mind Fitness walking. To do this, bring your attention to the action of walking. This present-moment focus can be on breathing, the sensations of walking—that is, how the earth feels beneath your feet, the touch of your clothes as you move, the overall sensation of movement—or on the entire sensory experience of walking, including the sights, sounds, and smells that are present. You can focus on one or all of these: we can be a breathing, walking body that is situated in a natural landscape. Whenever stories arise in the mind and compete for attention, bring attention back to the sensations and actions of the moment. Repeat as necessary.

Putting

FI is crucial to putting, perhaps more so than anywhere else in our game. Spend time developing your FI for the putting swing. As well, spend time producing a clear image of the putt you want to make. Actually see it in imagination following the trajectory it needs to get to the hole. *Feel* that image. Spend a lot of time making short putts. You want to have impeccable confidence in the two- to four-foot range. Also spend time putting to nowhere with no concern for making shots. Just work on developing the FI of your putting stroke.

Playing

Play at least one round alone once in a while. You can use this time of solitude to practice your Mind Fitness techniques without social distraction. Try to maintain mind FIT awareness throughout, returning attention to the action of *this* moment whenever it moves away. Make the round a sacred exercise of presence, an exploration of your very being as it moves in the ways we call golf. I suggest making this a regular habit.

FOOTNOTES

Acknowledgements: "Todd Trono …" Is the head pro at the Williston Golf Club in Williston Vermont/ "Scott Bevins …" Scott is a biomechanical expert.

Forward: "I was playing at my local course, The Links at Lang Farm …" The Links at Lang Farm is located in Essex Vermont. For more information visit http://www.linksatlangfarm.com. ‖. "I had the temerity and fortune to approach Steve "Gonzo" Gonsalves …" Gonzo is also the owner of Gonzo's Indoor Golf Club and Academy, located in Essex Vermont. For more information visit http://www.gonzosindoorgolf.com/. ‖ "I did so by using the Exquisite Mind Golf …" For more information on Exquisite Mind Golf, visit http://exquisitemindgolf.com/.

Introduction: "Conscious attention is like a flashlight …" This metaphor is provided by Jaynes 1976. ‖ "Estimates range to golf being 90% mental …" Morley 1976. ‖ "Harry Vardon suggested …" Penick 1992.

1. Mind Fitness: "Being distracted from relevant …" Perry 2005, 120. ‖ "Let's start with a topography …" I have borrowed the author and meditation teacher Shinzen Young's topographical model of the mind and his emphasis that mindfulness can be metaphorically understood as exercise for the mind and the benefits of mindfulness training include improved concentration, sensory clarity, and equanimity. I am indebted to Shinzen for the liberal use of these concepts. For more information visit http://shinzen.org/ and http://basicmindfulness.com/ "Mindfulness training, as a precise science of the subjective, is to human consciousness what the periodic table is to the material world" Shinzen Young, personal communication. || "To a less frequent degree ..." At an unconscious level we are always processing smell and taste information. We don't have to be consciously aware for this processing to happen. || "This mind tries its best to steer the brain ..." "The brain is made of 100 billion neurons. Each of these neurons can make up to 1,000 synaptic connections with other neurons, and each of these synaptic connections can be in a variety of electrical states. It is estimated that human brains are capable of entertaining 100 million trillion different thoughts. This is an incomprehensible number. Indeed, "Simple calculation shows that the number of humanly graspable sentences, sentence meanings, chess games, melodies, seeable objects, and so on can exceed the number of particles in the universe." Pinker 1997, 137. Furthermore, there are upwards of100 billion neurons in the brain, which is equivalent to the number of stars in galaxy. Each of these neurons may have from l1 to 1,000 synaptic connections (that is, connections with other neurons). This number now totals 1 quadrillion. Each of these synaptic connections can be in 1 to 10 electrical states. We are now talking about a number equivalent to 1 googol (1 with 100 zeros after it). This too is greater than the number of particles in the universe.

2. Too Many Minds: Appears in the film *The Last Samurai.* It comes during a scene where the character played by Tom Cruise is learning how to fight like a Samurai. He is chided, "Too many minds" when he is engaged in fighting self-consciously. || "William James, one of the founders ..." James 1911. || "Which mind will you bring to your next game? ..." When we play in the "zone," we naturally arrive in a state of Mind Fitness, or what we can call mindfulness. Mindfulness is something that we all have the capacity to experience and enjoy. Mindfulness is a native skill that can be developed through Mind Fitness to be more available and more responsive. This state of being is always present, yet often obscured by the clouds of mind activity. || "George Plimpton tells a wonderful story ..." Plimpton 1967.

3. Sensory Clarity: "Sensory clarity is a by-product of concentration. ..." In a personal communication with Shinzen, he explained that sensory clarity, "At a deeper level of understanding, clarity means a kind of soaking of awareness down into the neuronal circuits that create sensory experience. It's a sort of internally-generated functional MRI of your own nervous system—a deep knowing of yourself at a 'cellular,' that is, neuronal, level."

4. If You're Not Breathing, your Handicap is the Least of Your Problems: "If relaxation doesn't happen ..."

Once we can establish attention on natural breathing in the way just described, there are some advantages to learning how to breathe diaphragmatically (see Diaphragmatic Breathing in the Appendix).

5. **I Remember Now That I have Forgotten:** "How are you getting on with that memory-training ..." Shah 1988. || "We mostly live our lives asleep ...". Tart went on to say, "There is a social contract we implicitly live under. Most of us are asleep, are relatively mindless, are living in our waking dreams because that was the best we could do to protect against suffering, against the mindless assault on our essence when we were children. Someone who begins to show some signs of awakening can be very disturbing to people who are still heavily defended and deeply asleep." Tart 1994, 73.

6. Wi-Fi: "The pro Eddie Loos ..." Plimpton 1967. || "We all need to rest and recover ..." Loehr 2003. || "For a long time, it seemed as if ..." Murphy 2005, 138. || "Golfers have improved their game ..." Perry 2005, 124. || "The movement of the club ..." Wulf & Su 2007. || "Let's pause for a moment and think ..." To get the body and mind relaxed it can be essential to warm up before playing by running, stretching, sex, yoga, hot shower, juggling, or any other ritual that helps you to relax. Make sure that you remain hydrated and well-nourished as well. To practice WI-FI, take a relaxed promenade down the fairway. Don't fall into a tense focus. The orientation is like a wide-angle lens panorama with the FI in the middle of it. This is preferable to a hyperintense focus because the promenade gives the embodied mind a chance to recover between shots. The FI focus can bring moments of engaged rest. Can we learn something from elephant seals about engaged rest? They appear to be some of the laziest animals you can find. If you've ever seen them lounging on the beach or at Pier 39 in San Francisco, you would form this impression. However, oceanographers studying these creatures have found they spend 80 to 90 percent of their existence furiously swimming up to halfway across the Pacific Ocean in search of food (NOVA Ocean Animal Emergency). The lesson to take from these leviathans is: Work when you work and rest when you rest. Within sport psychology there is a growing recognition of overtraining (Peterson 2005). Athletes can exhaust themselves, physically and mentally, through the erroneous belief that more is always better. Training is best when periodic. Golfers can certainly get exhausted too and must take care to recover. Padraig Harrington won the British Open and then the PGA Championship in 2008 but faded from sight thereafter. He was exhausted and could not sustain that level of performance. In the course of a round we should also be mindful of rest and recovery--we all need both. In golf our task is to be acutely focused for the 1.7 seconds it takes to swing and the time that goes into our pre-shot routine. However, we should relax this focus once the shot has been executed. If we don't relax, playing golf will become draining and exhausting. Jack Nicklaus would engage in small talk between holes to recover from the intensity of his focus. If you like to talk, that's fine. I particularly enjoy doing mindful walking, paying close attention to the multiplicity of green hues, the wildlife, and flora on the course. As I approach the next shot, I make the transition into WI-FI preparation. I also enjoy juggling when there is a delay in playing. Juggling is an activity that engages my attention because it presents a sufficient challenge. One of my playing partners, who is an accomplished juggler, must juggle 5 balls at once to be feel challenged; I can get away with 3.

7. You Can't Think ... First Place: "If we could think of disastrous shots ..." Keefe 2005, 30. || "Mostly rumination ..." The brain and body undergo massive coordinated changes during a stress response. Stress can be caused by something as simple as getting vertical—standing up in the morning after a night's sleep. Stress can also arise after seeing a bear. In this more intense form of stress, the bodily changes are farther reaching. In order for something to be stressful we must interpret this event as a threat. For one person, the bear sighting is panic-stricken and overwhelming. He feels unprepared and ill-equipped to face the challenge. For another person, one with a camera around her neck, the sighting of the bear is an exciting opportunity—actually some of the same physiological changes might be present in the body but are interpreted differently. For a third person the bear sighting may be no big deal; he knows black bears are not dangerous and knows how to handle them. The situation for him does not outstrip his perceived ability to cope and therefore his stress response systems are not activated as they would be for the first individual. The stress "fight or flight" response prepares the body for action. There are changes in blood flow and energy through the body dictated by the release of neurotransmitters, neurohormones, and hormones. Here is a list of the changes that may occur (and how these changes help us to cope with threat):

- Pupil dilation (to help us to see better)
- Increased lung capacity (to help us to run better)
- Increased blood flow to the legs (to run)
- Decreased blood flow to the internal organs (digestion shuts down because it is no longer a priority; and if there is a wound to this vital area, reduced blood flow helps to prevent bleeding to death. In fact, all long-term projects are shut down, including digestion, growth and repair, and sexual functioning)
- Release of endorphins (to provide analgesia in case of injury)
- Increased blood flow to the brain (to help us be alert, problem-solve, and use memory to avoid harm)

The above "symptoms" are the action of the sympathetic nervous system, whose main product is adrenaline and cortisol with prolonged activation. If a threat is perceived as too extreme the system may shift to parasympathetic rebound and the organism freezes or faints. If the stress response gets severe, we will experience panic and additional symptoms may occur: palpitations, pounding heart rate, sweating, tremulousness, shortness of breath, a sensation of chocking, nausea or other gastrointestinal distress, dizziness or lightheadedness, pins and needles, restlessness, fatigue, muscle tension, and sleep disturbance (if prolonged). Along with these physical symptoms, individuals may have excessive and uncontrollable worry, a fear that they are going crazy or are about to die—in fact, some people having panic attacks present to emergency departments for fear that they are having a heart attack—difficulty concentrating or making decisions. Being familiar with how the body functions under stress can help us from magnifying the response. By keeping it manageable we can use the energy of the stress response to our advantage as discussed in Chapter 23 Desire is an Orange: Juice It.

8. Beware the Fine Print: "These categories can combine to form a mental model …" Bob Rotella refers to this as the unconscious self-image. Rotella 2001.

9 Fierce Attention: "The athlete who can focus on the task at hand …" Perry 2005, 113. ‖ "The golf swing has been described as 'controlled violence.'" Penick 1992, 70. ‖ "When we are both attentive and matter-of-fact

..." Young-Eisendrath 2007, 145. "Thinking that involves planning ..." I find, by contrast, that creative fantasy, such as composing writing, is not quite as perilous. ‖ "Mind Fitness practice does not just happen ..." We can use exercise as an opportunity to develop Mind Fitness. Don't read magazines or watch television; don't listen to music. It's easy to go on automatic pilot on a treadmill, stationary bike, or even road running or biking. Use these activities to train Mind Fitness. Train the mind while you train the body. I use my body training activities to train fierce attention, especially trail running, which I do several times a week with my Rhodesian Ridgeback. Trail running requires an intensity of attention. If my mind wanders from this intensity, I will get immediate feedback in the form of tripping over a rock or root. I must maintain a level of fierce engagement to remain safe. By doing so, my attention stays with breath and body sensations and perceptions of the running experience—the sights and sounds of being in the woods. If my mind moves from the present moment into a fantasy conversation, I am in trouble. These conversations may be actual conversations from the past that are remembered and regurgitated, or they may be rehearsals of conversations yet to come. In either case, the attention bandwidth required for maintaining them interferes with the performance of the present moment task of running through the woods. Thinking that involves planning also eats up too much bandwidth. I don't use an iPod when I run.

Instead, I use an "I" pod, allowing my embodied feelings in the present to be the focus of my attention. I listen to music before working out and then "hear" the music in the background as I run. The music functions as a score to the movie of the running experience. Like a good movie, the score should be present and set an emotional tone without being intrusive or explicit. ‖ "And his game would attest to this ..." Golf Week 15 November 2008.

10. Civilization Advances By ... Thinking About Them: "Civilization Advances ..." Alfred North Whitehead. ‖ "Self-consciousness explains much of why novices ..." Perry, 2005, 119. ‖ "Many things we do are done unconsciously ..." Students in my meditation classes sometimes feel that breathing can become self-conscious and temporarily difficult even though this function is controlled by the brain stem, the most primitive and thus automatic part of the brain. ‖ "An elevated certainty about future events ..." Keefe 2005, 26.

11. 100:1 "Our eyes for instance ..." Lakoff and Johnson 1999. ‖ "In this way, vision can be ..." New Yorker 30 June 2008, 63. "There have been some fascinating ..." To see a video, visit: https://www.youtube.com/watch?list=PLB228A1652CD49370&time_continue=51&v=vJG698U2Mvo&feature=emb_logo . A related episode of inattentional blindness occurred one day I was weeding a moss garden at a Japanese style Zen Temple. Hundreds of tiny weeds had grown up in the midst of a thick bed of moss perhaps 50 square feet in area. The area was also covered with pine needles. I happily set about my task. As I pulled the weeds and cleared the pine needles with my full attention they seemed to sprout up again as I worked. How could this be? It happens as the result of attention filtering—I thought I had cleared the patch but I was blind to some of the weeds. Attention as already discussed, while it appears to be complete, is not.

12. Amy G. Dala: "50,000 to 100,000 years ago …" "Indeed, For ninety-nine percent of human existence, people lived as foragers in small nomadic bands. Our brains are adapted to that long-vanished way of life, not to brand-new agricultural and industrial civilizations. They are not wired to cope with anonymous crowds, schooling, written language, government, police courts, armies, modern medicine, formal social institutions, high technology, and other newcomers to the human experience" Pinker 1999. || "On what we unconsciously know to be true …" Keefe 2003, 42. || "Ventromedial frontal cortex …" The ventromedial prefrontal cortex which interprets the activity of the amygdala; a fear reaction would start in the amygdala and limbic system and would then be modulated by the ventromedial and other parts of the cerebral cortex, going from primitive to more sophisticated.

13. Mirror, Mirror on the Wall: "Our brains are equipped with *resonance circuits* … "Siegel 2007.

14. See the Shot; Be the Shot: "When you are playing your best …" Plimpton 1967. ‖ "Imagery is used by a vast majority of athletes …" 90% of athletes at the Olympic Training Center used imagery. An overwhelming 97% of athletes and 100% of coaches judged such imagery practices to be effective. Imagery is also association-rich which facilitates learning. Murphy 2005. ‖ "Jack Nicklaus was reported to have said …" Keefe 2003. ‖ Imagery can be literal – imagining and rehearsing an event that will actually happen and imagery can also be symbolic. You might find some images help you to relax or help to energize your play. Such images are deeply personal and an image that works for one person may not work for you. ‖ "Gold medalist bobsledder …" These cases were reported in Murphy 2005. ‖ "'Putting to nowhere' …" Parent 2007.

15. 10,000 Hours or 10 Years, Whichever Comes First: "However, unless you've logged …" "We have shown that expert performance is acquired slowly over a very long time as a result of practice and that the highest levels of performance and achievement appear to require at least around 10 years of intense prior preparation." Ericcson et al. 1993. Ericcson's study was popularized by Malcom Gladwell as the *10,000-hour rule* in his book, *Outliers.* Critics of this rule point out that it is an oversimplification. Ericcson studied violin students who averaged 10,000 hours in the process of becoming experts, and as averages go, some did more and some did less.

Another issue is the type of practice: deliberate practice is better than mechanical repetition and practicing with an expert coach can make the most of the hours that are practiced. Genetics and a host of other factors play in as well. Ericcson et al. continue: "Chase observed that nobody had attained the level of an international chess master (grandmaster) with less than about a decade's intense preparation with the game." "Simon and Chase estimated that the amount of knowledge a chess master has acquired is comparable in size to the vocabulary of an adult native speaker of English. It takes normal individuals approximately a decade to acquire this vocabulary. Our review has also shown that the maximal level of performance for individuals in a given domain is not attained automatically as function of extended experience, but *the level of performance can be increased even by highly experienced individuals as a result of deliberate efforts to improve* (emphasis added). Hence, stable levels of performance after extended experience are not rigidly limited by unmodifiable, possibly innate, factors, but can be further increased by deliberate efforts. Instead, we argue that the differences between expert performers and normal adults reflect a life-long period of deliberate effort to improve performance in a specific domain." Ericcson et al. 1993. ‖ "Ben (Hogan) practiced thousands ..." Penick 1992, 130. ‖ "This rule states that ..." Peterson & Seligman,

quoted in Young-Eisendrath 2007, 95. ‖ "The beginner's mind is a jumble …" Keefe 2003, 36.
16. Tiger's Tibia: "Tiger Woods won the 2008 U.S. Open …" Ben Hogan pulled off a similar feat when he won the 1950 U.S. Open. He played this open just 16 months after a life-threatening car crash. "Hogan was three strokes ahead in the final round, but his legs throbbed in pain, and his caddie had to pick his ball out of the hole. Hitting his tee shot at the 12th, he nearly fell. He staggered toward Harry Radix, a friend who was standing nearby. 'Let me hang on to you, Harry,' he gasped, 'My God, I don't think I can finish.' On the second shot on the final hole, he hit one of the most famous shots in golf. With his familiar, precise swing, Hogan hit a low, boring shot that climbed to the top of a perfect arc and settled safely on the green, 40 feet from the hole. In agony, he two-putted for a tie." He later won the playoff. Barrett 2005. ‖ "Suffering and pain are not synonymous …" The meditation teacher Shinzen Young makes this distinction. Young 2005. "Understanding and responding to pain …" Some might imagine that being free of pain would be advantageous. If you could give up experiencing pain, would you? There are certain rare conditions that interfere with a person's ability to experience pain perception. Often as children, they destroy their skin and joints. These individuals have a foreshortened life span. We need the feedback of pain to remain intact and alive.

17. Affective Heuristics: "It can be helpful to make a distinction ..." The psychological literature on emotions and in psychiatric diagnosis confuses the terms feeling and emotion. Since we don't know in advance which choices will lead to survival and reproductive success, our system of feelings helps us to approximate and make the best guesses that we can. Brown & Kozak 1998. ‖ "Mind Fitness increases our attunement ..." Indeed, Mind Fitness or mindfulness can be thought of as a process of self-attunement. This relating to ourselves parallels parent-infant attachment and affects similar parts of the brain related to social intelligence and regulation of stress and emotions. Siegel 2007. ‖ "We want to be oriented bottom-up ..." The exception to bottom-up is when we need to strategize a shot; even here we want to be informed by bottom-up information: "Does the 5-iron *feel* more right than the 4-iron?" ‖ "Instead, if you are focused on relaxed feelings ..." Even a tense body will have relaxed feelings that can be found and focused upon. This holds even if your body is pain-ridden (see Appendix).

18. Perfectomy: "No person, athlete or not ..." Abrams & Hale 2005, 109. ‖ "Mind Fitness is like ... a 'perfectomy' ... The perfectomy concept was first presented in Kozak, Arnie, 2009, *Wild Chickens and Petty Tyrants: 108 Metaphors for Mindfulness.* Boston: Wisdom (later reprinted as *108 Metaphors for Mindfulness: From Wild Chickens to Petty Tyrants. 2015,* Boston: Wisdom). The distinction between perfectionism and curious gratitude reflects the distinction between ego-involved and task-involved athletes (Harwood 2005). Perfectionism is the domain of the ego. It is about creating a particular image of success. While there is no particular harm in generating images of success, how that image gets related to can become a problem. When that image becomes a *must* it becomes an albatross around our necks and drains our energy from performance. ‖ "Learning the difference between self-blame ..." Young-Eisendrath 2007, 76.

19. The Inner light: "Sport Psychologists have learned ..." Eliot 2005, 9. ‖ "It's not hard to imagine what happened next ..." From the story "The Man Who Quit" by Charles van Loan, 1914, reprinted in Halberry 1998.

20. Please Leave Your Ego, With Your Shoes, At The Door: "Please leave your ego ..." This quotation comes from the meditation and yoga master Swami Muktananda. As is the custom in India, students are expected to remove their shoes before meditation. He also advised his students to take off their ego too. ‖ "Everything is perfect ..." Quotation from the Zen Master Shunryu Suzuki Roshi. ‖ "Winning is a natural by-product of skill ..." Shooting well is a natural by-product of being in the moment just as relaxation is a natural by product of Mind Fitness. We don't aim for relaxation or for scoring, but aim for the process that can get us there. ‖ Research in sport psychology shows a task-orientation to be associated with more enjoyment, Harwood 2005, 26. ‖ "Ego-orientation makes us vulnerable …" Excessive ego-orientation can make us insecure. "A preoccupation with self-esteem makes us too self-centered, fearful, and worrisome. The result is too much focus on ourselves, competitive outcomes, and comparisons rather than on the performance task." Botteril 2005. ‖ "Ego orientation can be beneficial …" Harwood 2005, 33 notes the Competitive Performance Mentality (CPM) mind-set that reflects both task-and ego-involved goals, but it does so in a way that doesn't excessively pressure or coerce athletes to prove themselves to other people. He suggests exercises for imagining success such as the "Newspaper Article" that asks you to imagine how Golf Week would describe your victory. What are the task-oriented performance qualities that they'll report on? Envision composure, fluidity, accuracy, and consistency. ‖ "Researchers have also pinpointed …" Harwood 2005, 26. ‖ "It is said that the beginner's mind …" Suzuki 1970. ‖ "Task-oriented athletes use …" Harwood 2005. ‖ "Most golfers have bought into …" Perry 2005.

21. Freedom is Nothing More … Themselves: When I was in college, I coined the above aphorism. Once we've met our thermodynamic—that is, survival--requirements of having enough food and enough shelter not to freeze to death, our interests are driven by ego-based considerations. Many of these are fear- and shame-based. ‖ "To enjoy the aforementioned freedom ..." Researchers suggest that those who put their focus on controllable, or process-oriented, performance factors generally exhibit more tenacious effort. In other words, we are more likely to get discouraged and frustrated if we focus on outcome. "Dr. Bob Rotella urges his students to assign a low-level of importance to any given shot" Rotella 2008. ‖ "Most golfers have bought into ..." Perry 2005, 120.

22. Why Didn't I Kneel More Deeply to Accept You?: "Take discouragement, for example ..." Negative feelings like discouragement provide feedback that a goal cannot be reached and we would be better off investing our time and energy resources elsewhere. Nesse 2005. ‖ "We can't help but feel deficient ..." Sadness and anxiety are pandemic to modern life and the target of pharmaceutical interventions. Of course, sadness may indicate depression, which is a serious condition and anxiety may reflect an anxiety disorder. However not all anxiety and sadness are pathological and we run the risk of medicalizing the normal variations of human experience. ‖ "It doesn't get caught in the trap ..." For more recent sources on the science of happiness see Gilbert 2007, Ricard 2007, and Seligman 2003.

23. Desire is an Orange: Juice it!: "I had big nerves today." Carlos Franco was quoted after graduating at Q-School in 2007. ‖ "Certainly, he knew his skills ..." For some of us, we are predisposed physiologically to respond with more nervousness in clutch situations, or at least what are perceived to be clutch situations. This is an individual difference referred to as neuroticism in the research literature on personality. It is one of five basic dimensions of personality along with extraversion, openness to experience, agreeableness, and conscientiousness. The terms stress, anxiety, and arousal are often used interchangeably, but it can be helpful to make some distinction between them and to note their commonality (see the Appendix for a more detailed description of the stress response system, arousal, and anxiety). Stress can arise in response to physical challenges or arise in response to challenges that are perceived as either pleasant or unpleasant. Stress may be accompanied by the physiological changes we call arousal. Anxiety, as well, may or may not be accompanied by arousal. Fear is usually directed at specific target and anxiety is more general (although it can be hard to distinguish them at times). When anxiety or fear becomes extreme, we call this panic, and panic is accompanied by intense physiological arousal. || "A classic psychology experiment ..." Schachter and Singer 1962. || "we will have a better memory for negative outcomes ..." This makes sense from an evolutionary point of view. Those of our ancestors who were keyed into threat and interpreted potential threats at every turn, were more likely to actually detect and avoid threats, and hence survive and pass along their genetic material. Those of our ancestors who were too relaxed got eaten by the tigers because they weren't sufficiently threat oriented. We didn't get their genes because they got eaten. Instead, we got the hypervigilant ones! ‖ "Interpretation is key ..." If interpretation is responsible, this is good news because interpretations are not facts and are subject to revision. Balague 2005. This insight was made into a highly effective form of psychotherapy by Albert Ellis. It is called Rational Emotive Therapy and it seeks to examine and revise the interpretations we make about experience. ‖ "If there is no actual threat ..." A situation of actual threat would be getting stuck on the farthest reaches of the course in a thunderstorm; these systems of stress and arousal are designed to cope with these sorts of threats, not threats to your handicap. ‖ "We can play as if our lives depended upon it ..." Putting money on the line is a way in which many amateurs and pros train their focus. One pro I worked with devised a system of making payouts to causes they hated for losing, another was to make after work practice rounds "count" by putting a wager on the line—often in the form of a safe bet. In Rick Reilly's description of golfing for high stakes in Las Vegas, one of the contestants said, "I'm ruined for member guests at my own club and $20 games. You can't get it up for them once you had the adrenaline of these babies pumping through you. It teaches you *discipline of the mind* (emphasis added). If you start thinkin' of what you could lose, you wanna slit your throat." ‖ "One theory suggests ..." Balague 2005.

24. Different Day Different Body: "I like to do some juggling ..." If you can't juggle or are not interested in learning, find some other activity that can serve the same purpose. Richard Keefe untangles a length of string before playing his matches, which helps to get him quiet before playing.

25. The Whole is Greater than the Sum of the Parts: "violate the integrity of its wholeness ..." Wilber 2007.

27. Violent Emotion is a Kind of Insanity: "Violent emotion is a form of insanity ..." I am reminded of a Star Trek episode where a character says, "I agree with the Vulcans, violent emotion is a kind of insanity." Spoken by Dr. Miranda Jones from *Is There No Truth in Beauty?* Star Trek The Original Series. ‖ "We get suckered ..." This is an example of operant conditioning in action. This particular schedule of reinforcement is variable ratio and it explains the addictive power as slot machines. Learning that occurs in this way is very resistant to change. The brain having been rewarded on this random schedule never knows what to expect so keeps hope alive – "this next one could be *the* one!" ‖ "An angry, out-of-control ..." Abrams & Hale 2005. ‖ "While suppressing emotions is not healthy ..." Taylor 2006. ‖ "When we get angry and release it ..." This is the process of negative reinforcement in the learning theory of operant conditioning. Negative reinforcement means the cessation of something unpleasant that becomes reinforcing. The outburst removes the tension of the anger and is thereby reinforcing, making the outburst more likely to occur in the future. Negative reinforcement is often confused with punishment, which is an adverse consequence in response to a behavior. The neurohormonal changes that take place during anger such as the adrenaline rush and the release of endorphins may be reinforcing themselves leading to a condition of being addicted to our own emotions. || "Expressing anger physically, ..." Abrams & Hale 2005. || "Bill Parcels, put it this way, ..." Abrams & Hale 2005. || "Instead of being angry, be assertive ..." Abrams and Hale 2005. || My high school football coach was a case study in uncontrolled anger. Our football program was in disrepair and this new coach was brought in from a neighboring town with a successful football program to transform Marlboro High. I can recall our first game. I was a junior and on one of the first plays of the game, I was out of position on a punt. One of the assistant coaches chided me for being out of position and I tried to explain that it was someone else's fault (of course). The head coach overhearing me talk back to the assistant coach came over and starting screaming at me and slapping me across my facemask with his bare hand. In the retrospect provided by over 25 years and my having become a student of human behavior, I can see Coach's behavior as a form of—temporary--insanity. || "Lack of emotional control ..." Plimpton 1967. Further on the subject and quoting Dave Marr, Plimpton reports: "I've never seen a great golfer who didn't have a temper of sorts. But you control it. There's too much at stake. ... So you never see much more than a guy maybe whacking his club down once, digging the club head in a bit in the grass. Or, maybe, after a bad shot, he'll whip the club back in the bag awful quick." Plimpton 1967. One pro suggests that you don't put your club back in the bag until you are ready to let go of the shot.

28. Go With The Flow!: "This absorption lacks self-consciousness ...". "The elimination of excessive thoughts, doubt, and evaluation combined with a sense of effortless, timeless performance make for an incredibly pleasing experience—it's so intrinsic that athletes will chase flow independently of any other motivation variable." Eliot 2005. || "Flow is described as a rare and fleeting ..." For more on flow in sport see Jackson & Csikszentmihalyi 1999.

29. Kill Hope: "One recent article is instructive. ..." Golf Magazine, January 2009, Volume 51 (1).

30. Normal Curve: "The average golfers scores around 100 ..." The average score on an 18-hole regulation golf course was 98.3 in 2005. Average score was 96.4 for men and 108.1 for women. The percentage of adult golfers by score category are: Score under 80 (5 percent of golfers); 80-89 (19.7 percent); 90-99 (27.2 percent); 100-119 (32.8 percent); and 120 and above (15.3 percent). || "For the sake of this example ..." The standard deviation is a statistical measure of the degree of dispersion in a set of values. It helps to establish the parameters of the normal curve. ‖ "It takes a lot of work to move a handicap ..." "The purpose of the USGA Handicap System is to make the game of golf more enjoyable by enabling players of differing abilities to compete on an equitable basis. The System provides a fair Course Handicap for each player, regardless of ability, and adjusts a player's Handicap Index up or down as the player's game changes. At the same time, the System disregards high scores that bear little relation to the player's potential ability and promotes continuity by making a Handicap Index continuous from one playing season or year to the next."

32. Death Grip: "Since we were arboreal primates ..." Keefe 2005. ‖ "Likely, that effort ..." "Nothing inflates the vanity of a male hacker as much as bombing a huge drive" Hiaasen 2008. This reminds me of the Deadly Sin of Lust. Lust is the desire to go big. For men, especially, lust is a way of linking one's manhood with the length of his drives. Lust confuses effort with swing speed. We try harder but do poorer. A tighter grip slows the club speed. We miss the opportunity to play in a relaxed manner. Lust taps into the desire to make a good appearance on others. How often are we caught in this trap? It certainly feels good to crack a long drive, however, the driver is often not the best club choice. For high handicappers, Harvey Penick recommends putting your driver in the closet. At my home course, the 18th green is 350 yards from the back tees. A 20-yard gorse patch sits about 260 yards. To carry this, the drive must be in excess of 280 yards, perhaps a bit more. I cleared it once in a relaxed and inspired swing of the club. This was before I kept a handicap. Now I stand on the back tees trying to mount a score, the "risk" of trying to clear does not make sense. It's better to lay up with a 4-iron.

33. Set Up and Shut Up (or If You Think; You'll Stink): "With uncharacteristic resolve ..." Hiaasen 2008. || "The preshot routine can be likened ..." Cook 2006. || "Don't stand over the ball too long ..." I once tried to take an early season swim in Lake Champlain. It was early May and the water and air were still quite cool. I stood in the water up to my knees and tried and waited for a feeling of readiness to arise. I must have stood there for half an hour and still no feeling of readiness for diving into the cold that would steal my breath. I finally decided to be decisive. Go in or get out. I dove into the frigid lake water.

34. Your Wish is my Command: "The story of Mr. Poliwinkle ..." from the "Wooden Putter" by Bernard Darwin, in Halberry 1998, original publication 1924.

35. Slice Virus: "1/32 of an inch change in club face angle ..." According to Johnny Miller covering the 2008 Tour Championship.

36. The Ultimate Shot: "Life is a practice too. ..." Mind Fitness is also considered a "practice." One is never done. Even if we become enlightened, we keep training because it connects us to our most natural way of being.

38. Swing Like You Don't Care: "We become hostage ..." Jeff Silverman in his article "The Joys of Not Keeping Score." ‖ "freedom is eternal vigilance ..." after "The price of liberty is eternal vigilance ..." John Philpot Curran.

39. If You Aim at Your Target You've Already Missed: "There is traditional wisdom ..." For example, see Zen in the Art of Archery, Herrigal 1999. ‖ "David Cook presents a game ..." Cook 2006. ‖ "In order not to leave any traces ..." Suzuki 1970.

40. The Antidote to Exhaustion is Not Necessarily Rest: "Once you address the golf ball ..." Penick 1992.

42. Thank You: "Neuroscientists and positive psychology ..." As little as 15 years ago, the brain was believed to be much less plastic than we know it to be today. It was once believed that neurons did not regenerate but could form new connections. It is now known that neurogenesis is possible and that new connections form with great frequency.

43. Then They Still Have You in Prison: "Then they still have you in prison, my friend. ..." This story comes from Thich Nhat Hanh, the Vietnamese Buddhist monk who has run forgiveness and meditation workshops for Vietnam veterans. ‖ "We seek to re-orient ourselves ..." Harris et al. 2006.

48. The Great (Golf) Way ... no Preferences: The Third Zen Patriarch gave us the saying in the Tsin Tsin Ming: "The great way is not difficult for those who have no preferences ‖ "But, we protest, wouldn't we become zombies ..." Two images counter this zombie stereotype. The meditation teacher Larry Rosenberg tells the story of the Zen monk at the funeral who was openly weeping. After all, he had been friends with the newly deceased for many years. The second image comes from the cover of the Buddhist magazine *Tricycle* that shows a photograph of Tibetan Buddhist monks riding a roller coaster. Their arms are raised, and their faces are frozen in expressions of blissful exhilaration.

50. The Sharp Edge ... Salvation is Hard: "The Sharp edge of a razor ..." Maugham 1944. || "He speaks of having touched god ..." "Only my overwhelming sense of its reality. After all it was an experience of the same order as the mystics have had all over the world through all the centuries. Brahmins in India, Sufies in Persia, Catholics in Spain, Protestants in New England; and so far as they've been able to describe what defies description they've described it in similar terms. It's impossible to deny the fact of its occurrence; the only difficulty is to explain it. If I was for a moment one with the Absolute or if it was an inrush from the subconscious of an affinity with the universal spirit which is latent in all of us, I wouldn't know" – Larry Darrel from Maugham 1944. || "Rituals are often used in religious settings ..." Newburg et al. 2001.

51. The Perfect Doubt: "Let's not take doubts ..." Sogyal Rinpoche 1995. He continues: "Doubts cannot resolve themselves immediately; but if we are patient, a space can be created within us in which doubts can be carefully and objectively examined, unraveled, dissolved, and healed. What we lack, especially in this culture, is the rich, undistracted, and richly spacious environment of the mind, which can be created only through sustained meditation practice, and in which insights can be given the chance slowly to mature and ripen."

52. Opening the Gate: In the Zen Buddhist tradition, formal practice is marked by the symbolic creation of a gate. This is done through ritual. Bows are made to the Buddha adorned alter. Participants are not bowing to the Buddha image but to their own Buddha nature, that is, the capacity to be awake. Next, the Heart Sutra is chanted followed by more bows. This creates the gate through which formal meditation practice will take place. At the close of the formal sitting practice period, the gate is invoked again and closed. Such deliberate activity signals to the brain that we are about to do something important and significant. It wakes the brain up, invites it to pay attention to what is about to unfold.

54. 54: The first professional to break 60 was Al Geiberger who did so in 1977 at the Memphis Classic (29-30), Colonial Country Club. The others include: Chip Beck: 1991 Las Vegas Invitational (30-29), Sunrise Golf Club; David Duval: 1999 Bob Hope Chrysler Classic (31-28), PGA West (Palmer Course); Harrison Frazar: 2008 PGA Tour qualifying tournament; Paul Goydos, first round John Deere Classic; Stuart Appleby, fourth round of 2010 Greenbriar Classic;

Jim Furyk first round, 2013 BMW Championship; Annika Sorenstam: 2001 LPGA Standard Register PING.

Instructions for Mind Fitness Practices: "We can think of training Mind Fitness ..." These five components were developed by Shinzen Young, personal communication.

WORKS CITED

Abrams, Mitch, and Bruce Hale. 2005. Anger: How to Moderate Hot Buttons. In *The Sport Psych Handbook,* ed. Shane Murphy, 93-112. Champaign, IL: Human Kinetics.

Balague, Gloria. 2005. Anxiety: From Pumped to Panicked. In *The Sport Psych Handbook,* ed. Shane Murphy, 73-92. Champaign, IL: Human Kinetics.

Barret, David. 2005. *The Love of Golf.* Lincolnwood, IL: Publications International.

Botterill, Cal. 2005. Competitive Drive: Embracing Positive Rivalries. In *The Sport Psych Handbook,* ed. Shane Murphy, 37-48. Champaign, IL: Human Kinetics.

Brown, Terrance A., and Arnold Kozak. 1998. Emotion and the possibility of psychologists entering into heaven. In *What develops in emotional development?,* ed. Michael F. Mascolo and Sharon Griffin, 135–155. New York: Plenum Press.

Burns, George W. 2005. Naturally Happy, Naturally Healthy: The Role of the Natural Environment in Well-Being. In *The Science of Well-Being,* ed. Felcia Huppert et al., 405-434. Oxford University Press.

Chopra, Deepak. 2003. Golf for Enlightenment: The Seven Lessons for the Game of Life. New York: Harmony.

Cook, David. 2006. Golf's Sacred Journey: Seven Days at the Links of Utopia. Sacred Journey Stories.

Coyne, Thomas. Paper Tiger: An Obsessed Golfer's Quest to Play with the Pros. New York: Gotham

Eliot, John F. 2005. Motivation: The Need to Achieve. In *The Sport Psych Handbook,* ed. Shane Murphy, 3-18. Champaign, IL: Human Kinetics.

Ericcson, K. Anders, Ralf Th. Krampe, and Clemens Tesch-Romer. 1993. The role of deliberate practice in the acquisition of expert performance. *Psychology Review* 100 (3): 366–406.

Gilbert, Daniel. 2007. *Stumbling on Happiness.* New York: Vintage.

Hallberry, William. 1998. *Perfect Lies: A Century of Great Golf Stories.* New York: Touchstone.

Harris Alex, H. S., Frederic Luskin, Sonya B. Norman, Sam Standard, Jennifer Bruning, Stephanie Evans, Carl Thoreson. 2006. Effects of a group forgiveness intervention on forgiveness, perceived stress, and trait-anger. *Journal of Clinical Psychology* 62(6): 715-733.

Herrigel, Eugen. 1999. *Zen in the Art of Archery.* New York: Vintage.

Hiaasen, Carl. 2008. *The Downhill Lie.* New York: Knopf.

Horn, Thelma. 2008. *Advances in Sport Psychology.* Champaign, IL: Human Kinetics.

Jackson, Susan & Csikszentmihalyi, M. 1999. F*low in Sport: The Keys to Optimal Performance and Experience.* Champaign IL: Human Kinetics.

James, William. 1911. *Some problems in philosophy.* New York: Longmans Green.

Jaynes, Julian. 1976. The Origins of Consciousness in the Breakdown of the Bicameral Mind. New York: Houghton Mifflin.

Keefe, Richard. 2003. *On the Sweet Spot.* New York: Simon & Schuster.

Kozak, Arnold. 2009. Wild Chickens and Petty Tyrants: 108 Metaphors for Mindfulness. Boston: Wisdom Publications.

Lakoff, George & Johnson, Mark. 1999. *Philosophy in the Flesh.* New York: Basic.

Loehr, Jim & Schwartz, Tony. 2003. *The Power of Full Engagement.* New York: Free Press.

Maugham. W. Somerset. 1944. *The Razor's Edge.*

Morley, David. 1976. *The Missing Links: Golf and the Mind.* New York: Tempo.

Murphy, Michael. 1972. *Golf in the Kingdom.* New York: Delta.

Murphy, Shane (Ed.). 2005. *The Sport Psych Handbook.* Champaign IL: Human Kinetics.

Murphy, Shane. 2005. Imagery: Inner Theater Becomes Reality. In *The Sport Psych Handbook,* ed. Shane Murphy, 127-154. Champaign, IL: Human Kinetics.

Nesse, Randolph N. 2005. Natural Selection and the Elusiveness of Happiness. In *The Science of Well-Being,* ed. Felcia Huppert et al., 3-34. Oxford University Press.

Newberg, Andrew, D'Aquili, Eugene & Rause, Vince. 2001. *Why God Won't Go Away: Brain Science and the Biology of Belief.* New York: Ballantine.

Parent, Joe. 2002. *Zen Golf: Mastering the Mental Game.* New York: Doubleday

-- 2007. Zen Putting: Mastering the Mental Game on the Greens. New York: Gotham.

Penick, Harvey. 1992. *Harvey Penick's Little Red Book.* New York: Simon & Schuster.

Pepper, Stephen. 1942. *World Hypotheses: A Study in Evidence.* University of California.

Perry, Clark. 2005. Concentration: Focus Under Pressure. In *The Sport Psych Handbook,* ed. Shane Murphy, 113-126. Champaign, IL: Human Kinetics.

Peterson, Kristen. 2005. Overtraining: Balancing Practice and Performance. In *The Sport Psych Handbook,* ed. Shane Murphy, 49-70. Champaign, IL: Human Kinetics.

Pinker, Steven. 1997 *How the Mind Works.* New York: Norton

Plimpton, George. 1967. *The Bogey Man: A Month on the PGA Tour.* New York: Lyons and Burford.

Ragonnet, James. 2007. Golf's Three Noble Truths. The Fine Art of Playing Awake. Novato, CA: New World Library.

Rilke, Rainer Maria. 1989. *Selected poetry of Rainer Maria Rilke.* Ed. and Trans. Stephen Mitchell. New York: Vintage International.

Rinpoche, Sogyal. 1995. *Glimpse After Glimpse.* San Francisco, CA: Harper.

Reilly, Rick. 2003. *Who's Your Caddy?* New York: Doubleday.

Ricard, Matthieu. 2007. Happiness: A Guide to Developing Life's Most Important Skill. New York: Little, Brown.

Rotella, Bob. 2001. *Putting Out of Your Mind.* New York: Simon & Schuster.

-- 2008. Your 15th Club: The Inner Secret to Great Golf. New York: Free Press.

Seligman, Martin. 2003. Authentic Happiness: Using the New Positive Psychology to Realize Your Potential for Lasting Fulfillment. New York: Nicholas Brealey.

Schachter, S. and J. E. Singer. 1962. Cognitive, social and physiological determinants of emotional state. *Psychological Review* 69, 379-99.

Shah, Idries. 1989. The Exploits of the Incomparable Mulla Nasrudin/The Subtleties of the Inimitable Mulla Nasrudin. Octagon Pres.

Suzuki, Shunryu. 1970. *Zen Mind, Beginner's Mind.* Boston: Weatherhill.

Tart, Charles. 1994 *Living the Mindful Life.* Boston: Shambhala.

Taylor, Shelly. 2006. *Health psychology.* Boston: McGraw Hill.

Whyte, David. 1999. *Fire in the Earth.* Langly, WA: Many Rivers Press.

Wilber, Ken. 2007. *A Brief History of Everything*. Boston: Shambhala.

Wulf, Gabriele, and Jiang Su. 2007. An external focus of attention enhances golf shot accuracy in beginners and experts. *Research Quarterly for Exercise and Sport* 78(4), 384-389.

Young-Eisendrath, Polly. 2008. *The Self-Esteem Trap*. New York: Little & Brown.

Young, Shinzen. 2005. *Break Through Pain*. Boulder: Sounds True.

Made in the USA
Columbia, SC
06 June 2021

39261610R00102